Cathryn J. Wellner

D0603625

THE HOT & SPICY COOKBOOK

Other books by Moira Hodgson

THE CAMPUS COOKBOOK

CHINESE COOKING WITH AMERICAN MEALS

COOKING WITH FRUITS AND NUTS

QUINTET: FIVE AMERICAN DANCE COMPANIES

THE RAW FOOD COOKBOOK

MOIRA HODGSON

THE HOT & SPICY COOKBOOK

ILLUSTRATED BY HELEN LEW WEEKLEY

McGRAW-HILL BOOK COMPANY
NEW YORK ST. LOUIS SAN FRANCISCO
TORONTO MEXICO DÜSSELDORF

Book design by Lynn Braswell.

Illustrations by Helen Lew Weekley.

Copyright © 1977 by Moira Hodgson
All rights reserved. Printed in the United States of America.
No part of this publication may be reproduced, stored in a retrieval system, or transmitted, in any form or by any means, electronic, mechanical, photocopying, recording, or otherwise, without the prior written permission of the publisher.

1 2 3 4 5 6 8 9 MUBP 7 8 3 2 1 0 9 8 7

Library of Congress Cataloging in Publication Data

Hodgson, Moira.
The Hot and spicy cookbook.
Includes index.
1. Cookery, International. 2. Spices.
I. Title.
TX725.A1H55 641.6'38'3 76-52464
ISBN 0-07-029143-8

CONTENTS

For my parents

My thanks go to the
Moroccan National Tourist Office and to
Hassan Esserghini, Mary Jarrett, Elizabeth Tingom,
Raeford Liles, and Bully.

INTRODUCTION

It is hardly surprising that Americans have taken so readily to hot, spicy cooking. Food shops in "foreign" neighborhoods, with their burlap bags of beans, jars and boxes of spices, dried chilies, exotic fruits and vegetables, dried and pickled fish, piles of nuts and roots, are delightful places to whet the appetite and discover new ingredients. Abroad, the *souks* of Morocco, the open markets of Mexico, the bazaars of India and the Far East, all tempt even the most amateur of cooks. The warm, musky aroma of dried spices piled high in bins captures the imagination. Turmeric, tamarind, aniseed, mustard seed, cumin, bay leaves, pepper, cardamom, saffron—their vivid colors wait to be scooped up by the vendor and shoveled into newspaper cones which are dropped into your shopping basket. Small boys hawk bunches of fresh coriander and mint and the scent catches you as you pass and makes you ponder over fish, shrimp, or chicken. Then there are the chutneys, pickled lemons, glistening olives, peppers, oranges, tomatoes, strings of onions—all these add to the fascination of spicy food.

Columbus's search for a spice route to the Indies led him to the continent of America, where he found the capsicum plant that yields the fiery little peppers that now appear in hundreds of varieties all over the world. To follow their journey is to trace the voyages of discovery and trade. This chapter is but a cursory glimpse into the cooking traditions that have developed around chili peppers, an indispensable feature of the goulashes, *sambals*, *satés*, and curries of these pages.

The biggest chili-eating region of the United States is the Southwest. Chilies are not only used in Mexican dishes, they are added to corn bread, potatoes, beans—even to spaghetti sauces. The food of this dry, rolling country is a combination of frontier cooking (barbecued ham, beef, sausages, spareribs, chicken, and steaks) and Mexican/Indian, which is based on corn, beans, chilies, peppers, squash, and tomatoes. Tex-Mex food is richer in meat and cheese than Mexican but features such Mexican specialties as *tamales* (steamed corn husks filled with corn dough and meat), *chiles rellenos* (large, spicy green peppers stuffed with cheese and fried in an egg batter), *chorizos* (hot sausages), and, of course, *tortillas* combined with different fillings and appearing as *enchiladas*, *tacos*, and *quesadillos*.

Chili con carne (chili with meat) is a Tex-Mex triumph. Its ingredients are as variable as the traditional stew. It is generally accepted, however, that the genuine version should contain beef cubes, dried chilies, oregano, and cumin simmered with a little water. Cornmeal is sometimes used to thicken the sauce. (Mexican *chili con carne* is a thinner version, often made with meat other than beef.) One of the best Texas chilies I've had contained beer and bitter chocolate. The hamburger-chili-beans variety most often sold in cans is unacceptable to any purist.

In addition to beans, which are eaten throughout the Southwest (simmered with chilies and onions, sometimes mashed with scallions, peppers, and cumin and tossed in oil and vinegar), chick peas are a popular vegetable. They were brought to the continent by the Spanish. They can be mashed and baked in a soufflé; cooked with meat and chilies; or simmered with slices of *chorizo* and diced chili.

Mexican immigrants in California introduced turkey *mole poblano*, a holiday dish and one of the most remarkable inventions of Mexican cooking. The sauce is made from a combination of almonds, chilies, raisins, tomatoes, onions, garlic, sesame and pumpkin seeds, sugar, bread, tortillas, herbs, cinnamon, and cloves with bitter chocolate, all ground and simmered in stock until thick. The result is dark, spicy, and rich—you can't taste the chocolate but the sauce is not the same without it. There is a legend that it was invented by a group of nuns in the Santa Rosa convent in Puebla. When the archbishop paid them a surprise visit they had nothing to offer him for dinner. So they prayed for inspiration and, guided by heaven, they went into the convent kitchen and ground or chopped all the edibles they had. Then they slaughtered the convent turkey and put it into the pot. The archbishop was, of course, delighted.

This famous story is probably apocryphal. According to Elisabeth Lambert Ortiz, an authority on Mexican food, *mole poblano* is typically Aztec. The Spaniards reported seeing clay pots filled with a rich dark sauce simmering in the market places on their initial visit to Mexico. *Mole* powder is now available, but most Mexicans view it with scorn and prefer to grind their own spices.

Cuban and Puerto Rican immigrants have made an important contribution to American cooking. Frequently served specialties include black beans; fried plantains with pork crackling; *ropa vieja* (literal translation: old clothes), shredded beef in a thick, reddish brown sauce; and *sofrito*, a rich garlicky tomato sauce, popular throughout the Caribbean and often used to flavor soups and stews. Cubans have also brought their own version of *arroz con pollo*, using chilies, olives, and capers where the Spanish used artichoke hearts, asparagus tips, and beans.

The Chinese settled in Cuba in great numbers and a fascinating new cuisine grew up. Cuban-Chinese immigrants to the United States have opened flourishing restaurants in New York and Florida. A meal may begin with black bean soup laced with rum. Subsequent courses may consist of fried rice, Chinese vegetables, fried plantains, and *picadillo*—chopped beef cooked with olives, raisins, tomatoes, and peppers. *Picadillo* was probably a Moorish dish brought over by the Spaniards, tomatoes and peppers being the Cuban contribution. Black beans and rice is another Cuban dish which reveals its history in its name, *Moros y Cristianos* (Moors and Christians).

Immigrants from Hungary have also made an impact on American cooking. Hungarians invented the magical combination of lard, onions, and pure ground paprika that so impressed Escoffier that he introduced two Hungarian dishes into the *grande cuisine* of France: Hungarian goulash and chicken paprikash.

While Indians used the chili pepper whole and the Spaniards mixed it with spices, the Hungarians were the first to use their version of the chili pepper, a descendant of the American capsicum known as paprika, in powdered form unmixed with anything else. Hundreds of varieties of paprika peppers grow in Europe and they vary from hot to sweet. In the Balkans, people grind the dried peppers and use them in stews or sauces, or slice them fresh and serve them with chopped onions in oil as a side dish. They also use paprika to spice sausages and ham.

Most of the major cities of the United States have excellent restaurants serving a cosmopolitan cuisine, but the town with the highest reputation for its food is New Orleans. Creole cuisine is a blend of Choctaw, French, Spanish, and African.

Miles of inland waterways teeming with crayfish, and the long coastline with oysters, crabs, shrimp, and pompano make New Orleans especially good for seafood. The culinary term *creole* has come to mean a spicy concoction of tomatoes, green peppers, onions, and garlic. Cayenne and Tabasco peppers were brought north to the port of New Orleans by the Spaniards, along with spices from Latin America and the Caribbean. One of the most famous Louisiana specialties is gumbo (the name comes from the African word for okra), halfway between a soup and a stew. A highly seasoned *roux* is its basis—to which are added scallions, herbs, and a choice of either shellfish (oysters, crayfish, or shrimp) or meat (chicken, veal, or ham). The most important ingredient is filé powder, first used by the Choctaws, which is made from ground sassafras leaves and thyme.

One of the best meals I've ever had was along the River Road between New Orleans and Baton Rouge. I stopped for lunch on a cold, gray day at an unprepossessing little truck-stop café. There was no choice—you took what the proprietor served. I began with a steaming bowl of seafood gumbo and went on to large, succulent crayfish stuffed with herbs and spices in a light tomato sauce. The meal ended with wonderful black Louisiana coffee.

The Spanish conquistadors were astonished when they arrived in Tenochtitlán (now Mexico City) to find an extremely sophisticated Aztec cuisine. Bernardino de Sahagún, a Spanish priest who was there at the time, wrote of ". . . white fish with yellow chili; gray fish with red chili; frogs with green chili; newt with yellow chili; lobster with red chili, tomato, and ground squash seed; white fish with a sauce of unripened plums; tamales made with honey . . ." Over a thousand dishes were served at the court of Montezuma and many of these have remained unchanged to this day. *Tortillas*, *tamales*, *tacos*, and *quesadillos*; dark, spicy sauces; corn, beans, squash, pumpkin, peanuts, manioc, vanilla, cashews, cacao (the basis of chocolate), avocados, papaya, sweet potatoes, pineapple, and turkey were staples. The conquistadors introduced oil, wine, onions, garlic, chicken, cinnamon, cloves, rice, wheat, peaches, apricots, pigs, and cattle (and subsequently butter and milk).

Although Mexican food is often fried in lard, it is never greasy when properly cooked. Among the more interesting specialties are *huevos rancheros* (eggs fried and served with beans, chili sauce, and tortillas); *guacamole* (mashed avocado with tomatoes, onions, chilies, and lime juice, served with tortilla chips); *pescado yucateco* (fish Yucatán style, cooked with pimientos, chilies, olives, and orange juice). When I was in Yucatán I ate shrimp cocktail almost every day. It was not the tired mixture of overcooked shrimp with bottled tomato sauce that often passes in restaurants, but an arrangement of very fresh, cold shrimp on a plate with chopped onion, tomatoes, chilies, and fresh coriander and an olive oil and lime juice dressing.

At dusk in Chiapas, where I lived, in highland Maya country, the aroma of frying *quesadillos* would float up the hill. These are tortillas folded over a piece of cheese and fried until the outside is crisp and brown and the cheese is melted inside, which my neighbor would cook over a charcoal brazier and sell from her doorway to people in the street. She always spooned hot red *salsa* on top. Throughout Latin America *salsa* is as indispensable on the table as salt and pepper in other countries. It is often made from raw or cooked tomatoes, with peppers, spices, onions, and chilies and used as a dipping sauce. The hottest table sauces are found in Yucatán.

Farther south, the long coastline of Central America yields an abundance of fish which is often cooked with tropical fruits and vegetables such as bananas, coconuts, oranges, limes, and lemons, combined with chilies.

South America is dominated by the Andes, which stretch for 400 miles from Venezuela almost to the foot of the continent, parallel to the Pacific coast. The food is partly African, partly Moorish, and tropical, but most of all Indian–Aztec, Incan, and Mayan.

The potato was developed in Peru, where the Incas flourished until the Spaniards arrived. The Indians invented a method of drying potatoes by slicing them very thin and exposing them to the freezing mountain air day and night until the moisture evaporated. Ordinary potatoes are mashed with cream cheese, olive oil, and chilies (known in Peru as *ají*). *Ají* is related to the Mexican chili but it has a different flavor. Among outstanding Peruvian dishes are *ají de gallina* (chicken simmered in a spicy sauce made from chilies and walnuts) and *ceviche* (fish, scallops, or shrimp marinated in lime or lemon juice with garlic, onion, and chilies). The fish turns white, "cooked" by the lemon juice. *Anticuchos*, a close cousin to the Indonesian *saté*, are a form of kebab made from beef heart cut into small cubes, threaded on skewers, and marinated in chilies, garlic, and orange juice. It is grilled over hot coals. I made it often in Mexico and served it with a sauce of coriander, raw onion, and orange juice. It is delicious—and very cheap.

A Bolivian specialty is *picante de pollo*, a hearty chicken stew made with garlic, onions, sweet peppers, thyme, marjoram, and *locato* (the local chili pepper). One-dish meals called *chupes* resemble the French *pot au feu* except that they contain substantial amounts of chili which helps the Indians keep out the mountain cold.

Less chili is used in Colombia and Venezuela than in Peru and Bolivia, although the Spanish influence has given the food a piquant taste. *Pabellon* (spiced shredded beef) is similar to *ropa vieja* and served with fried plantains and rice. In Caracas you can get excellent beef grilled and served with a hot peppery table sauce; along the Venezuelan coast, fish is often cooked in coconut milk. Food in Chile, Argentina, and Uruguay is more European and generally not as spicy as it is in Mexico, Brazil, and parts of Central America.

Brazilian cooking has a totally different character than the rest of South American cooking. It is predominantly a mixture of Indian, Portuguese, and African ingredients. Manioc, a root crop, was the principal staple of the Indians. Corn, sweet potatoes, and peanuts were probably imported from other parts of Latin America; bananas, coconuts, yams, and okra were brought over by African slaves. The food has a distinctive yellow-orange color brought about by the use of dendê oil (palm oil) which is sold in varying shades from red to pale yellow all over Brazil. Malagueta pepper, from the east coast of Africa, is also used as a seasoning. The pepper actually originated in the Americas and was taken to Africa and brought back again. The most famous cooking in Brazil is Bahia, which shows a strong African influence. Fish and shrimp are cooked in dendê oil with nuts, ginger, and peppers, or simmered in coconut milk. Hearts of palm is a popular salad (fresh hearts are *quite* different from canned); cassava meal is sprinkled over fish, meat, and poultry.

Like other Latins, Brazilians are fond of table sauces; in their version, called *môlho de pimenta*, both chilies and malagueta peppers are used. The country's national dish, *feijoada completa*, originated in Rio de Janeiro. Dried and smoked meats, including dried beef, tongue, fresh beef, pork, bacon, sausage, corned spareribs, and pig's feet are arranged on a platter and served with collard greens, cassava meal, sliced oranges, and *môlho de pimenta e limão*, a dipping sauce made from chilies and lemons.

The cooking of the Caribbean is extremely eclectic. The islands, colonized by the Spanish, French, Portuguese,

Dutch, British, and Danish, frequently changed hands. But what gives Caribbean food its distinctive flavor is the use of indigenous island produce such as mango, guava, plantain, pineapple, coconut, breadfruit, cassava, and fresh seafood, including lobster, crayfish, conch, and shrimp.

The food is characterized by tomatoes and chili peppers, a taste which goes back to the original inhabitants, the Carib and Arawak Indians, who were using chilies probably brought over from Yucatán when the Spaniards first arrived. The Arawaks also grew cassava, yams, sweet potatoes, corn, guava, cashews, and pineapples. They were hunters and lived on game and fish. Europeans brought oil, wine, vinegar, oranges, limes, lemons, rice, and coffee. During the years of the slave trade, between the mid-sixteenth and mid-nineteenth centuries, a totally different cuisine came into being. The Africans introduced okra, an important feature of the Creole gumbo, and a penchant for spicy seasoning. Cinnamon, ginger, nutmeg, allspice, and cloves combined with chilies and peppers, have become important components of Caribbean cooking. Meat is often marinated before it is cooked and simmered in a sauce containing chilies, onions, garlic, tomatoes, coriander, and thyme.

When the slaves were freed in the mid-nineteenth century, many of them preferred working in the sugar-cane fields to remaining servants. There was a demand for new labor which came this time from China and India. And so two more cuisines were introduced.

The Chinese brought their methods of cooking and growing vegetables; the Indians brought rice, curries, and chutneys. Most islanders use a curry powder which they mix themselves. Kebabs and pilaffs are also now part of local cooking. A typical Caribbean table today might include kebabs, a curry, rice, and Chinese vegetables along with chutney, fried plantains, and grated fresh coconut.

In Guadaloupe I have eaten *poisson en blaff*, which is prepared with a mixture of French and island cooking techniques: red snapper is marinated in lime juice and chilies, then simmered in white wine with malagueta peppers and chilies. In Trinidad I have had conch curry and the smallest, sweetest oysters I have ever found anywhere served with a peppery sauce delicate enough not to mask their flavor. I also remember a spicy chicken soup in Aruba cooked with pumpkin, sweet potatoes, corn, beans, peas, and red peppers. It was just the thing after a long morning swim.

West African food is similar in many ways to Caribbean but it is generally "hotter." Dishes as colorful as the local handicrafts are cooked in orange dendê oil with tomatoes, red chilies, green peppers, and onions. Fish from the Atlantic coast is plentiful. It may be fresh, dried, salted, or smoked. Peanuts are frequently used to thicken sauces—chicken is stewed in coconut milk with ground peanuts, garlic, onions, peppers, and tomatoes; shrimp is served in peanut sauce flavored with crushed chili peppers. Sauces are also thickened with mashed yams or a purée of black beans, potatoes, plantains, or grated coconut.

Africans are extremely inventive with yams, pounding them to a paste called *fufu* which is served with grilled meat and stews. They also make them into croquettes and chips, or mash them with crushed chili peppers or freshly grated nutmeg.

Meat in Africa usually has plenty of flavor but tends to be tough since most farm animals are free-ranging. It is often marinated before being cooked. A popular marinade in Senegal is known as *yassa*. Lemon juice, chopped onions, chilies, salt, and pepper are mixed together and poured over the meat, which is left to stand in the mixture for a couple of hours.

Jollof rice, an African specialty much like paella, is eaten all over the continent. Meat or chicken is marinated in lemon juice with garlic, tomatoes, and onions, then browned and cooked with tomatoes, garlic, chilies, and ginger. The rice is stirred in and cooked at the end. *Jollof* rice is served with hardboiled eggs, spinach, or cabbage.

A combination of African and Portuguese cooking has developed in Angola and Mozambique. Mint, cinnamon, cloves, saffron, coriander, cumin, and red peppers are popular aromatics. Shrimp is eaten frequently, cooked in olive oil and coconut milk with chilies, coriander, tomatoes, and onions. Chicken is stewed with cashew nuts and served with coconut rice.

Piri-Piri, a fiery table sauce, is eaten with steak, lamb, chicken, fish, and shellfish. Tiny fresh red chilies are simmered in lemon juice, removed, and pounded to a paste. The sauce keeps well and is the African counterpart to *salsa*.

South African cooking is a curious mixture of Dutch and Southeast Asian. Moslem immigrant workers from Java, Sumatra, and Malaya have brought with them a cuisine similar to that of Pakistan, introducing kebabs, curries, chutney, *sambals*, *biryanis*, and *blatjangs*. They also brought a knack for pickling and preserving fish. Fish is sliced and fried in oil, then preserved in a mixture of chilies, turmeric, homemade curry powder, ginger, brown sugar, bay leaves, and wine vinegar. Other Moslem-inspired dishes include *bobodie*, a spicy mincemeat pie made with ground lamb seasoned with curry and lemon juice; and *sosaties*, cubes of lamb marinated in onions, curry powder, chilies, garlic, and tamarind water and cooked like the *shashlik* of the Middle East—skewered and roasted over an open fire with the marinade used as a sauce. *Bredie* is a South African goulash spiced with ginger, chilies, cinnamon, and cloves.

Farther north, Ethiopians are fond of a fiery seasoning called *berbere* which is used on grilled or raw meat or as a flavoring in stews (known in Ethiopia as *wat*). Each cook has his own special way of preparing it. Red chili peppers are dried and pounded in a mortar. Ginger, garlic, and onions are ground with cloves, cinnamon, nutmeg, cardamom, allspice, fenugreek, peppercorns, and coriander.

North African food is less hot but very spicy. Cinnamon, cumin, saffron, turmeric, ginger, black pepper, Cayenne, aniseed, paprika, and sesame seed are used in the food of the Maghreb people who live in Morocco, Algeria, and Tunisia. *Couscous* is the national dish of the Maghreb. A fine semolina, made from wheat grain, is steamed over a lamb or vegetable stew. Chick peas, onions, carrots, zucchini, peppers, eggplant, leeks, raisins, and celery might be included in this stew. The vegetables are cut into large pieces and arranged at the bottom of a *couscoussière*, seasoned, and covered with water. The steam that rises from their simmering cooks the semolina, which is placed in a perforated pot over the top. *Couscous* can be served with *harissa*, a pungent pepper sauce which, when thinned with olive oil, is used with brochettes or served on olives or with salads. While Moroccan *couscous* is generally flavored with saffron, Algerians use tomato purée and the Tunisians make a very spicy sauce with chilies and ginger.

The last time I had *couscous* was something of a celebration. I was with friends in Marrakech. We had noticed women (newlyweds) whose hands and feet were painted with henna—the result was like a beautiful, deep-rust, lacy tattoo. We wanted to try it on ourselves. The henna women arrived at the house in giggles and we lay under the vine leaves on cushions, drinking mint tea while they painted. We had to remain there for several hours, immobilized until the henna dried. Meanwhile the women, in a festive mood, prepared a *couscous* which they brought to us on a low table. Since we could not use our hands (or even stand up), they had to feed us, rolling *couscous* deftly into balls and putting them into our mouths. We drank Oustalet, the splendid Moroccan rosé, and one of the women, although a Moslem and not supposed to drink, mixed hers with Coca Cola, half and half, and four teaspoons of sugar.

I have always loved Indian food. As children living abroad we used to have curry lunches—it was "not done" to eat curry in the evening, I can't remember why. Several different kinds of curry would be served buffet-style on a large table with small bowls of condiments—chutneys, *rayta* (yoghurt dishes), chopped apples, bananas, raisins, coconut, peanuts, tomatoes, onions—and various kinds of bread. It was an Anglicized version, of course, but it always looked and smelled so good. At boarding school we would eat curry once every two weeks. Those we considered the weak and feeble would ignore our jeers and be served ground meat in gravy at the "mince" table. At the curry table we were served the hottest beef curries I have ever had. An Indian would probably have been horrified. The sauce was thickened with flour and certainly made from commercial curry powder, but I thought it was delicious. I always felt excitement on those days when, after morning classes, as we lined up in compulsory silence to file into the dining room, I would smell the rich aroma down the hall.

The traditional use of curry (which comes from the word *kari*, meaning sauce) grew out of a need to preserve meat in extreme heat. There are hundreds of different kinds from hot to mild, and traditional recipes vary greatly from region to region. The heart of all Indian cooking is the *masala*, the combination of spices which gives each dish its special flavor. *Masalas* may be "wet," spices ground with vinegar, water, or coconut milk (the base of dishes in the south) or "dry" (more commonly used in the north). Combining the spices correctly is a skill and the sign of a good cook. Basic spices include turmeric, a hard yellow root which is ground into a fine powder; cumin seeds, whole or powdered; coriander seed; fenugreek; fennel seed; and saffron. Poppy and sesame seeds, nutmeg, cardamom, cloves, and cinnamon are common aromatics; chilies, onions, garlic, and fresh herbs such as coriander, mint, and basil are also frequently used. Lemon juice, vinegar, and tamarind water, pomegranate seeds, and dried mango powder give added piquancy to Indian food.

Religion has had a major impact on Indian and Pakistani food. The predominantly Hindu population in India is vegetarian and their food is generally "hotter" than Moslem. Vegetables (known as *bhaji* in the north, *foogath* in the south) are commonly fried in spices with no sauce. Curries are made with one or more vegetables. Sometimes vegetables are shaped into patties and fried. Moslems in Indian and Pakistan eat plenty of meat—mainly beef, lamb, and chicken. They never eat pork. Specialties include *koftas* (spicy meatballs), *kormas* (braised meat cooked in yoghurt or cream), *kebabs*, and *bhoonas* (meat sautéed, then baked). Pakistani specialties include *shami kebabs* (curried meatballs), chicken *tikka* (grilled chicken), shish kebab, and beef *biryani*.

In Northern India, bread making is an art. Excellent breads accompany every meal and they are used to scoop up the thick, dry sauces. They are often spiced. Among the most impressive are *naan*, unleavened bread which is baked in a tandoor, a five-foot-deep clay jar oven; *chapattis*, unleavened griddle bread; *paratha*, a multilayered spongy bread; *poori*, deep-fried puffs; and *pappadums* made from lentil flour.

One of India's finest dishes is chicken *tandoori*. The chicken is marinated for a day or two in yoghurt and spices, then broiled in a tandoor oven, which gives it a crisp exterior while keeping it tender and moist inside.

Southern Indian sauces, more liquid than northern sauces, are generally eaten with rice. Particularly good are *vindaloo* dishes (lamb, chicken, or shrimp marinated in a combination of vinegar, spices, and chili peppers and simmered in the marinade). Coconut oil is the popular cooking fat. In the north *ghee* or clarified butter is used, and Bengalis prefer mustard oil.

Yoghurt is eaten by Moslems and Hindus alike to aid digestion. It is often served plain or combined with diced vegetables and spices. *Dahl* (lentils), of which there are nearly sixty varieties in India, are stewed and served as an antidote to hot curries.

Although the Indonesians share the Indians' penchant for curries, the distance covered by the 3,000 islands is responsible for interesting variations in Indonesian cuisine. Among the islands with a distinct culinary reputation are Java, Sumatra, Kalimantan (previously Borneo), Silawesi (Celebes), and Bali. Javanese food reflects its agricultural background. Sumatran dishes were created as a result of the heavy trade in spices and are liberally seasoned with dry seeds and aromatic spices. It was these spices—nutmeg, cloves, and mace as well as turmeric, pepper, ginger, and cinnamon—that were exported to Europe and the Middle East, where they altered the character of local cooking.

In Indonesian cooking today, the Arabs, Chinese, Spanish, and the Indians have all exerted their influences. Curries in Indonesia have fewer spices than their Indian counterparts. Coconut milk, chilies, onions, and turmeric are the basic ingredients. Flavoring agents include lemon grass, *laos*, *blachan*, or *trassi* paste (a shrimp paste), garlic, coriander, limes, citrus leaves, and cumin. A popular condiment to be found on almost every table is *ketjap*, an Indonesian soy sauce.

When the Dutch gained control of the Indonesian spice market, the *rijstaffel*, a feast of Indonesian dishes, became the symbol of Dutch colonialism. *Rijstaffel* is an awe-inspiring spread which may consist of twenty to thirty Indonesian specialties—fresh pineapple slices, fresh and fried bananas, dried shrimp, chopped peanuts, grilled meat, curries, *krupuk* (pounded shrimp fried in hot batter which puffs into curly flakes), mango chutneys, and various *sambals*. *Nasi goreng* (fried rice with chicken) is often served with heavily spiced fish, with accompaniments of cucumber relishes, gherkins, and fresh coconut. *Saté*, small chunks of meat or fish, are threaded onto wooden skewers, marinated and basted with soy sauce and oil, cooked over charcoal, and served with a pungent peanut sauce. To complement these divergent flavors, the Indonesians serve side dishes of raw or cooked salads and yellow rice cones decorated with chilies.

Another mélange of Chinese and Indian cuisines, with the emphasis more on the Chinese, exists in Malaysia and Singapore. Chilies in vinegar or fresh, chopped red chilies are frequently used as a garnish. Thai cooking is similar to Javanese—composed of many artfully decorated curries and Chinese dishes, with ingredients similar to those used by the Indonesians.

In the neighboring Philippine Islands, the cuisine has a distinct Spanish overtone. Food is less "hot"—*paellas*, sweet-sour stews, and grilled fish are typical.

The cooking of China ranks with the French as the finest in the world. There are five noted schools: Peking, Canton, Foochow, Hunan, and Szechwan. Spices are used to enhance the flavor of food, not to mask it. Sesame oil, hoisin, plum, oyster, and soy sauces, dried mushrooms, bean paste, star anise, fermented black beans, Szechwan pepper, dried shrimp, and cloud ears (a dried fungus) are the most frequently used seasonings. Food is cooked in oil with garlic, scallions, and fresh ginger. The emphasis is on harmony and accent. Sweet is cooked with sour, crunchy with smooth; ingredients are seldom cooked alone, but combined to bring out the best in each other.

Cooking time is short for Chinese dishes; the preparation takes much longer. Ingredients are chopped in advance and cooked fast so that they retain their freshness. More pork is used than beef and the meat is generally cooked with vegetables. Few dairy products are eaten; vegetables and rice are the mainstays of a meal. Barley and wheat are also often used. Chinese vegetable cookery is the best in the world. It brings out the flavor and texture of the vegetables without destroying vitamins.

Although most Chinese dishes are cooked according to certain basic principles, China is such a vast country that there can be variations in local ingredients which give the impression of regional specialties. The inland province of Szechwan produces a pepper called *fagara*, a crop which is partly responsible for the hot, spicy food for which the region is famous. Food is cooked in oil with the pepper, which may not always seem fiery at first, but develops its heat almost as an aftertaste. Besides *fagara*, chilies are a major flavoring agent, as are garlic, scallions, Five Spices (a ground blend of *fagara*, star anise, aniseed, cloves, cinnamon), dried mushrooms and other fungi, ginger, and fennel.

Although there are no religious taboos preventing the Chinese from consuming lamb, it does not often figure in the diet. Pork, chicken, game, and fish from local rivers are the usual choices. Meat is often smoked or barbecued. Sometimes it is twice-cooked (first simmered and then stir- or deep-fried). The most renowned Szechwan dishes are duck or pork; chicken with walnuts or hot peppers; spiced meat in a sauce delicately flavored with dried tangerine peel; hot and spicy carp; and pork with (imitation) fish flavor.

Hunan cooking is even "hotter" than Szechwan. The Yellow River running through this province is famous for its carp, which is served in a spicy sweet-sour sauce or in a hot bean sauce. Dry shredded venison in hot sauce is another popular Hunan dish.

Perhaps the widespread awareness of the insipidity of refined, mass-produced food has contributed to the trend in America toward highly seasoned cooking. When one is confronted with foods which have so little taste or flavor—vegetables grown for size, not quality; meat reared on hormones; standardized eggs—spices become almost indispensable. Even the most rural supermarkets have begun to stock spices and chilies on their shelves.

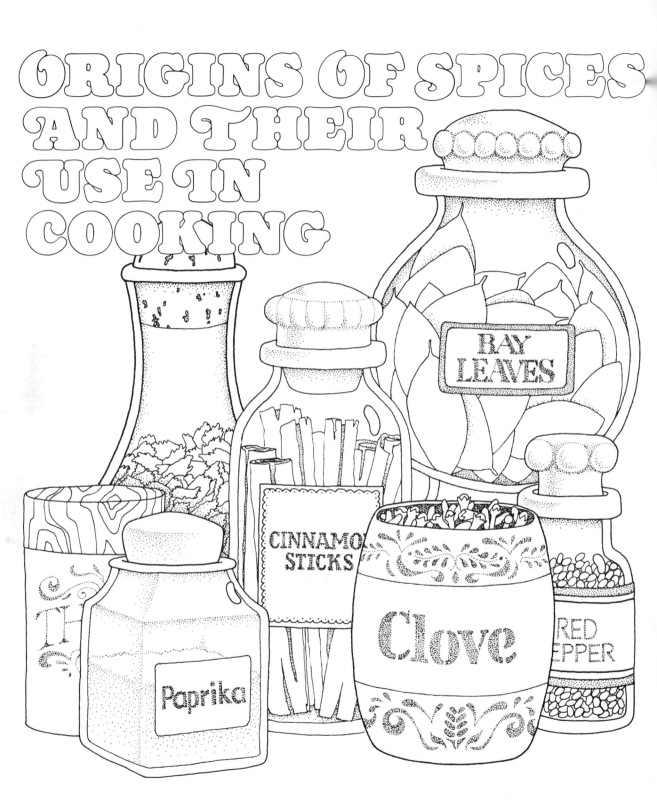

ORIGINS OF SPICES AND THEIR USE IN COOKING

ANISE

Anise is native to Middle Eastern countries. The seeds come from a plant with long, feathery leaves, and taste of licorice. They are a natural stimulant and help counteract gas. Anise is said to aid the digestion and was used at the end of a meal by the Romans for such a purpose. Indians also employ the seeds as a pleasant-tasting *digestif*.

Anise is used in curries, stews, cheese dishes, and with fish.

ALLSPICE

This is not a mixture of spices, as some people believe. It is the berry of the allspice tree, which grows in the West Indies. Bought whole, and freshly ground with a pepper mill, it has a stronger flavor than in its packaged, powdered form.

It is a pungent and aromatic spice, tasting like a mixture of cinnamon, cloves, and nutmeg. It is used in curries, Mexican dishes, and goes with most beef, lamb, and chicken stews.

CARDAMOM

Cardamom originates in India. It is the dried fruit of a plant belonging to the ginger family and one of the chief ingredients in curry powders. It has a strong, cool flavor and is mentioned in Sanskrit writings as preventing bad breath, headaches, fevers, coughs, colds, nausea, and even eye diseases. The greenish or straw-colored pods are usually discarded and only the tiny dark seeds inside are used in cooking. Cardamom is also very popular in Scandinavia. It was brought to Scandinavia from Constantinople by the Vikings and has been used there ever since.

Cardamom is used in preparing Indian food; it enhances fish, chicken, and fruit dishes. Arabs also use it to flavor coffee.

CAYENNE

Cayenne pepper consists of the ground seeds and pods of peppers which originally came from Cayenne in Africa. It helps the digestion. A small amount is excellent with egg and cheese dishes, sauces and shellfish.

CINNAMON

The cinnamon tree is native to Ceylon and Malabar. The pungent fragrance of its bark comes from the oil, which has valuable uses in medicine. It is a stimulant, a carminative, and an astringent. It is also a preservative.

Cinnamon is used in many Southeast Asian, Indian, and Mexican dishes and in desserts and fruit sweets.

CLOVES

The clove tree is an aromatic evergreen which looks rather like a laurel. It grows principally in the Philippines, Molucca Islands, and Zanzibar. The dried, unopened flower buds were used to preserve foods in the Middle Ages and to mask the taste of rotting meat.

Cloves are a powerful antiseptic; they also sweeten the breath. Sanskrit writings describe the use of cloves against fever and stomach ailments, to stimulate the heart, and to help the functioning of liver and kidneys. They were also used as a local anesthetic, especially for toothache. Cloves help digestion by accelerating the flow of gastric and intestinal juices.

They are used in Indian and Mexican cooking, tomato, meat, and fish sauces, in soups and stews, and with fruit.

CORIANDER

Coriander spices many Mexican, Indian, and Indonesian dishes. It is native to southern Europe and the Near East. The plant has lacy leaves and looks like flat-leaved parsley.

The dried seeds have a fresh, delicate aroma which is best brought out when they are ground in a pepper mill immediately before use.

Coriander is another basic ingredient in curry powder.

CUMIN

Cumin seeds are small and yellow brown. They look and taste very much like caraway. Cumin is used for curry powders, chili powders, and in Middle Eastern, Mexican, Indian, and North African cooking. Although available ground, the seeds are better bought whole and pulverized with a mortar and pestle. They are a valuable aid to the digestion.

Cumin is also good in bread, with cheese, eggs, meatballs,

and hamburgers, in pilaff and other rice dishes. It is an interesting complement to chicken, lamb, and eggplant.

FENUGREEK

Fenugreek is a tiny reddish brown seed that has a slightly bitter flavor and a sweet spicy scent when heated. It can be used powdered or ground.

Fenugreek too makes an important contribution to the characteristic flavor of curry powder and is a feature of many Indian dishes.

GINGER

Ginger is a root (or rhizome) used widely in Indian, Chinese, African, Caribbean, Mexican, and Southeast Asian dishes. It is one of the most ancient spices, said to have originated in south Asia and the East Indies. In its dried, powdered form, ginger is more pungent than when it is fresh. Jamaican ginger has a more delicate flavor and is by many considered the best.

An ancient remedy for warding off colds, ginger is a stimulant, carminative, and stomach remedy. Sanskrit writings mention it as a cure for anemia and liver complaints.

Fresh ginger is sliced or chopped into stews and Chinese dishes. It complements fish, meat, and poultry.

HORSERADISH

The piquant, biting taste of the horseradish root gives mustard its characteristic flavor. Freshness is essential in horseradish as it is apt to become bitter if kept more than a season. Its sharpness is a pleasant contrast to fatty meats.

MACE AND NUTMEG

Mace is the outer coating of the seed which grows on nutmeg trees in Ceylon, Sumatra, and Malaya. The Spice Islands, once under Dutch control were the original source of nutmeg. The Dutch, to preserve their monopoly on this valuable spice, dipped the nutmegs in lime so that the English and French would not be able to plant the seeds.

Sold in powdered form, mace is mild and fragrant. It can

often be substituted for nutmeg, although its flavor is somewhat stronger.

Nutmeg is best freshly grated—in the old days little nutmeg graters were worn around the neck by people who could afford the exotic spice. With cheese, vegetables, and curries it is subtle yet definite. Nutmeg is a reputed stimulant; known as a cure for colic, flatulence, and an aid to digestion.

MUSTARD

Mustard is an annual herb. It grows in Europe, Asia, and North Africa. The seed can be dark red or yellow. Whole mustard seed is not as hot as ground mustard. Commercial powdered mustard is often a blend of both, sometimes turmeric is added to heighten the yellow. Prepared mustard is a paste made with vinegar or wine, sugar, and herbs. In some intangible way, mustard ingredients reflect national temperaments. French mustard is usually mixed with white wine or vinegar, German with tarragon vinegar and spices, English mustard, like Chinese mustard, is a paste made from plain mustard powder mixed with water.

In sauces, with meats, fish, vegetables, and pickles mustard is popular seasoning.

PAPRIKA

Paprika comes from a species of capsicum cultivated in Central America, parts of Europe, and the United States. The pepper was taken to Europe by Columbus, who discovered it in the Caribbean islands.

Hungarian paprika is the most renowned; it is the strongest and consists of the whole pod, seeds, and stems of the dried red pepper. A mild Spanish paprika is the one most commonly used in the United States. Its *raison d'être* is color and garnishing.

Paprika is the only known dry source of Vitamin C and a tablespoon is said to equal the juice of four lemons. Recent research has found paprika to be high in carotin, vitamins A, B, B_2, and Vitamin P, which is important in the prevention of arteriosclerosis. Paprika stimulates the appetite, increases the flow of gastric juices, and has been used in treatment of bronchitis, pleurisy, joint and nerve afflictions.

PEPPER

Black pepper, often confused with peppers of the capsicum family, is a berry which grows principally in India, Southeast Asia, and the East Indies. In the Middle Ages it was a source of wealth and was used to pay taxes. Henry II imposed levies of pepper, which in those days approached the value of gold or silver. The Portuguese monopoly on the pepper trade lasted well into the eighteenth century.

Pepper comes in several forms: powdered, coarsely ground, and whole peppercorns. White pepper is merely pepper with the outer coating of the seed removed. The innovation of white pepper was esthetically inspired: to some people black grounds in a white sauce are as distressing as black tar on a white beach.

SAFFRON

Saffron is the dried stigma of an autumn crocus, native to Asia and parts of Europe. It is the most expensive spice in the world. Over 200,000 stigmas are needed to make a pound. It has a warm, bitter aroma and a golden color and is sold powdered in small envelopes or in tiny orange and gold threads. Some of these powders are adulterated with turmeric. Saffron rice is a popular dish in Indian and Asian cooking. The spice is also used in stews and curries.

One of the earliest known spices, saffron was very popular in Europe and used by the Babylonians, the Greeks, and the Indians. In medieval England it was used as a hair dye. Bhuddist monks use it to dye their robes.

In ancient and medieval times, saffron was thought to revive the spirit, and to prevent fainting fits and palpitations of the heart.

TURMERIC

Turmeric is native to India and other parts of Asia. It is a dried aromatic root or rhizome related to the ginger family. The brilliant yellow of turmeric varies in hue from canary to saffron. Moroccan dishes get their characteristic color from turmeric, which is an ingredient of curry powder (also used in sauces and rice).

SOME ORIENTAL FLAVORING AGENTS

Fish Sauce: A bottled sauce available in Chinese markets, containing fish extract, water, and salt. It is useful for flavoring soups, stews, and sauces.

Ketjap Manis: This is an Indonesian soy sauce, sweeter than the Chinese variety.

Laos: Available whole or in powdered form in Indonesian specialty stores; laos is the root of a Malayan plant related to ginger.

Sereh or Lemon Grass: An aromatic, lemon-scented tropical grass, available dried as a powder or in blade form, and fresh in Hawaii and Puerto Rico.

Trassi: A thick Indonesian shrimp paste, trassi has a strong smell and keeps almost indefinitely. It should be stored in a closed container.

CHILI PEPPERS

CHILI PEPPERS

Within a century after their discovery in the New World, peppers and chilies altered the character of national cuisines. Used as vegetables or spices, peppers and chilies are of the capsicum family. Hundreds of varieties range from mild and sweet (the bell pepper) to fiery (Hungarian paprika capsicum). Red peppers are green peppers that have matured on the vine. Red chilies, most frequently sold dried, produce quite a different effect from the green ones, which are available fresh or canned.

Both red and green chilies are used in the native cuisines of Mexico, Indonesia, Malaysia, Thailand, India, Pakistan, parts of Africa, and China. They have a high vitamin content and are often munched whole. The Peruvian Indians of the Andes have a chili so hot that the smallest quantity will transform an otherwise bland dish.

Chilies are essential to certain relishes, chutneys, *sambals*, and Latin American hot sauces. Few of the recipes in this book insist on a particular variety except in cases where a recipe simply would not be right with a substitute—Mexican *mole poblano*, for example. In these instances powdered, canned, fresh, or dried chilies are specified. The following is a list of chilies generally available in the United States; most of the names are in Spanish.

DRIED RED CHILIES

These are wrinkled and should be stored in a jar away from the light.

Ancho A mild, medium-sized chili, most commonly used in Mexican cooking and irreplaceable in certain sauces.

Cayenne A long, thin pepper, very hot and used to make Cayenne pepper.

Chipotle A small, bright red chili that is often sold pickled.

Guajilla A long, narrow, light red, mild chili.

Hontaka A Japanese chili, longish, medium sized, and red hot.

Mirasol Colorado A fairly large, mild red chili, widely used in Peru.

Morita A small, very dark, hot chili, available canned as well as fresh.

Mulato A brownish red chili. Very dark, pungent, and longer than the *ancho* chili, it is indispensible for certain Mexican sauces. This and the *ancho* chili are sometimes confused and called *pasilla* chilies.

Pasilla Also known as *chili negro* in California. It is a long, slender chili, a very deep red, almost black, and has less flavor but more bite than *ancho* and *mulato* chilies.

Pequín A tiny, red hot chili, used dried.

GREEN CHILIES

Jalapeño A fairly large, hot chili, available fresh and canned in California and the Southwest.

Largo A long, thin, yellowish green, hot chili.

Poblano Resembles a bell pepper, sometimes hot but usually fairly mild. Available both fresh and canned in California and the Southwest.

Serrano A smallish, tapering chili, quite hot, available fresh and canned.

SWEET GREEN PEPPERS

Guero A California green pepper, light yellowish green and quite mild. It is used fresh and is available throughout the United States.

Valenciano The sweet green bell pepper (also available red) sold fresh throughout the United States.

Preparing Chilies

To prepare fresh chilies, run them under cold water and cut off the tops, remove the seeds and the veins if they are large. They can be peeled and scraped after charring over a gas flame, and then wrapped in a towel. This makes them soft for cooking in sauces and enhances their flavor.

Dried chilies should be torn into small pieces and soaked in boiling water for half an hour before being used. About 1 cup of water to 6 chilies is the usual proportion (this applies only to recipes using dried chilies that are not ground to a powder). The chilies are then put in a blender with their soaking liquid and puréed.

Chili powder is a blend of ground seeds and pods from dried chilies mixed with other herbs and spices such as cumin, garlic, oregano, and Cayenne pepper. See page 42 for Homemade Chili Powder. The powder you buy varies a lot in potency. Do not keep powders for over a year—they lose their vitality. A spice grinder comes in handy for dried chilies, it quickly reduces them to a fine powder. A tablespoon of powdered chili equals 1 whole chili. Cayenne can be used in place of *chili pequín*. *Ancho*, *mulato*, and *pasilla* chilies are available in powdered form in specialty shops.

Pepper flakes are made by grinding dried red chilies very coarsely, usually with the seeds.

To reduce the strength of a chili, remove the seeds. Fresh chilies can be made milder by being soaked in salted water for a while before being used.

Canned chilies should be rinsed in cold water to remove the brine.

You can sting yourself if you touch chilies with your bare hands and then touch your mouth, eyes, or nose. For this reason it is advisable to wash thoroughly with soap and water after handling chilies.

THE
HOT & SPICY
KITCHEN

EQUIPMENT

It *is* possible to live without a corn popper or a waffle iron. There are, however, certain items that should be included in every kitchen. The following is a basic list.

Pots and Pans

Use a heavy, cast-iron frying pan or the French kind with a copper bottom. Cast-iron pans need not be washed if the food has not been cooked in animal fat (this includes, of course, butter). They can be wiped out with paper towels and salt. Iron pans should be left overnight with a layer of oil in them before they are first used; otherwise they may get rusty.

Casseroles made from enameled cast iron are the best although the very large ones can be extremely heavy. Cast-iron casseroles are particularly versatile since they can be used both on top of the stove and in the oven.

Unglazed pottery casseroles with tightly fitting lids, available in French specialty stores, Mexican shops, and in Morocco (where they are known as *tajins*) are excellent for stewing. They, too, should be soaked with oil before they are used.

A wok is not an essential piece of equipment but it is extremely useful, particularly for stir-frying food. It is a round, concave pan and it should be washed and carefully dried after being used. Do not fill it more than a third full when you are using it or the food will spill out when you stir.

A steamer is excellent for cooking vegetables. A simple fan-shaped insert usable with most saucepans can be bought for very little in dimestores. This can also be placed in a deep-frying pan. A collapsible salad basket will serve this function too. A spaghetti cooker or a *couscoussière* will also perform the double duty of steaming vegetables.

Knives

A cleaver is good for chopping vegetables. French cleavers are smaller than Chinese and not quite as menacing. Knives should be kept very sharp. The flint method is the most effective. Carbon steel knives keep their points better than stainless steel but they have a tendency to rust.

Other Equipment

A slotted spoon is good for removing food from sauces or water.

A set of measuring spoons and cups. Aluminum is more efficient than plastic.

A bulb baster. Again, aluminum is better than plastic, which tends to melt at the tip.

Iron trivets are prettier and safer than asbestos mats under pans to prevent food from burning. Incidentally, avoid thin aluminum pans and glassware because they burn food unless carefully watched.

A set of wooden spoons.

A wire whisk.

Mixing bowls in assorted sizes.

A butcher's block or thick chopping board, which should be placed near the stove.

Plenty of washable potholders.

A roasting pan with a rack.

A blender or food mill for making purées. A mortar and pestle or small spice grinder for spices.

An oven thermometer.

A meat thermometer.

KITCHEN HINTS

How to Prepare Tomatoes and Green Peppers

Roll the whole tomatoes or peppers over a gas flame until the skin is charred all around. Tomatoes can be peeled immediately. Peppers should be wrapped in a dishcloth and left for a few minutes. Unwrap, peel off the skin, cut in half, and remove the seeds. Then chop or leave halved, according to recipe.

Tomatoes can also be peeled after being dropped into boiling water for a couple of minutes. I prefer the charring method since it gives the tomato a charcoal flavor.

Using Herbs

Put fresh herbs into a cup and chop them with a pair of kitchen scissors.

Powdered herbs have less flavor than crumbled leaves. Store away from light.

Fresh basil, tarragon, rosemary, and thyme can be grown in small pots on a kitchen window sill. Chives are the only herbs that take well to freezing. Basil can be frozen and used in stews but it loses much of its flavor and the color goes off.

Chopping Garlic

Smash the garlic with the skin on with the flat side of a knife. Then peel and chop.

If you choose to use a garlic squeezer, leave the skin on the garlic. When you come to clean it, lift out the skin (the garlic will have been pressed through, leaving the skin inside) and you will find that the bits of garlic that generally get stuck in the holes of the press will come out with it in one piece.

Using Gingerroot and Horseradish

Both of these can be frozen. Peel them and wrap them in foil. Grate while frozen hard.

Salt

Sea salt or rock salt ground in a small wooden grinder is the best. Kosher salt is good too.

Seeds and Nuts

Sesame seeds are delicious baked dry in the oven and sprinkled on food.

Ground pumpkin seeds, almonds, hazelnuts, walnuts, pine nuts, and sesame seeds are excellent as sauce thickeners.

Breadcrumbs

These can be made in the blender with toasted or fresh bread and stored in the refrigerator in a jar. Toast can also be turned into breadcrumbs if you put it in a paper bag and hammer it with a rolling pin.

Oil

The best sesame oil is Chinese. Health-food stores sell a variety without much flavor. This, along with light oils such as safflower or other nut oils are the best for frying foods when you do not want a dominant oil flavor.

POWDERS, PASTES & BASICS

I once came across a letter in the food section of a newspaper in which a woman complained that the food editor always asked for freshly ground pepper in her recipes. "I am a busy housewife," she wrote, "and I do not have time to grind pepper every time I cook." One wondered why she bothered to cook at all and what kind of meals she must have served. She was missing one of the most enjoyable aspects of cooking. There is great satisfaction in grinding spices or pounding them with a mortar and pestle, smelling the rich aroma that rises as their oil is released.

Spices can be ground in a blender or small spice grinder. Like coffee, they lose their oil and flavor if left for a long time after they have been ground. A small pepper mill will grind coriander seeds, mustard seeds, and allspice successfully although it will not reduce them to the fine powder some recipes demand. Whenever possible, one should buy spices whole and grind them at home.

Curry paste should not be used as a substitute for curry powder, but only where specified in the recipes. Curry powder is not a spice, as some people still believe, but a blend of spices. The powder usually contains, among other ingredients, turmeric, coriander, mustard seed, allspice, and chili. Indian families grind and mix their own, making it mild or hot as they please. Commercial curry powder varies, but by and large it has a harsh medicinal taste and is made with inferior spices.

This chapter also includes simple chili pastes and powders, recipes for spiced oils and vinegars and mixed ground spices, some of which can be made and stored until needed. It also includes a section on staples for certain spicy recipes such as coconut milk, homemade yoghurt, ghee, tamarind water, and so on, which are referred to throughout this book.

MADRAS CURRY POWDER

4 dried red chilies
4 tablespoons coriander seed
5 tablespoons cuminseed
2 tablespoons peppercorns
3 tablespoons turmeric
½ teaspoon mustard seed
½ teaspoon fenugreek
2-inch cinnamon stick
6 cardamom seeds
2 tablespoons cloves

This is a hot, pungent curry powder.

• Combine the ingredients in a blender or spice grinder and grind until fine.

MILD CURRY POWDER

1 tablespoon turmeric
2 tablespoons ground mace
2 tablespoons ground cloves
4 tablespoons peppercorns
2 tablespoons peeled cardamom seeds
4 tablespoons cuminseed
2 bay leaves
1 dried red chili

• Roast all the ingredients for half an hour in a 200-degree oven. Grind in a spice grinder or blender.

GARAM MASALA

½ cup peeled cardamom seeds
2 tablespoons ground cinnamon
¼ cup ground cloves
4 tablespoons ground mace
4 tablespoons coriander seed
¼ cup peppercorns
3 tablespoons black cumin

This is an aromatic powder which can be used as a basis for curries or for marinating meat. It can also be sprinkled on food just before you serve it.

• Roast the cardamom seeds in a 200-degree oven for half an hour without browning. Remove the pods and combine in a blender or spice grinder with the remaining ingredients. Grind very fine.

SIMPLE GARAM MASALA

• In a blender or grinder combine ¼ cup cloves, ¼ cup peppercorns, 3 tablespoons peeled cardamom seeds, and 1 tablespoon cinnamon. Blend well.

MASALA WITH CHILIES • In a blender or grinder combine 2 dried red chilies, ½ cup coriander seed, a tablespoon cumin, and 2 tablespoons turmeric. Turn the mixture out onto a piece of foil and bake in a 250-degree oven for about half an hour.

THAI CURRY PASTE

4 dried red chilies, ground, or 4 green chilies, chopped, pages 27–29
2 shallots, chopped
1 garlic clove, chopped
1 tablespoon trassi (shrimp paste), page 24
1 teaspoon laos powder, page 24
1 tablespoon sereh powder, page 24
1 tablespoon paprika
1 teaspoon cuminseed
1 teaspoon coriander seed
Grated rind of one lemon
Coarse salt

A medium-hot paste. It can be made in a blender or with a mortar and pestle, the dry ingredients being ground first and made into a paste with the juice from the shallots and chilies.

• Combine all the ingredients in a blender and purée. If using green chilies, omit the paprika.

INDIAN CURRY PASTE

4 dried red chilies
4 tablespoons coriander seed
1 tablespoon cumin
2 tablespoons black pepper
2 tablespoons coarse salt
1 tablespoon mustard seed
½ tablespoon saffron soaked in 3 tablespoons hot water
1 clove garlic, crushed
½ cup vinegar
¼ cup ghee or butter

This will keep better if you use ghee, page 45, instead of butter. It is a fairly hot paste.

• Grind all the dry ingredients. Combine in a blender with remaining ingredients and mix to a smooth paste.

INDIAN VINDALOO PASTE

- 1 *medium onion, coarsely chopped*
- 2 *cloves garlic, coarsely chopped*
- 1 *tablespoon turmeric*
- 2 *tablespoons coriander seed*
- 1 *teaspoon ground chilies*
- ½ *teaspoon mustard seed*
- ¼ *teaspoon fenugreek*
- 1 *teaspoon ground ginger*
- 1 *teaspoon cuminseed*
- *Vinegar to make a paste*

This paste makes a hot, sweet-sour curry.

• Put the onion and the garlic in the jar of an electric blender or chop finely and put in a mortar to grind with pestle. Grind the spices in a spice grinder and combine with the onion mixture. Add enough vinegar to make a paste and blend, adding more vinegar, if needed, to make a thick, stiff paste. Use as directed in recipes.

INDONESIAN VINDALOO PASTE

- 6 *green chilies*
- ½ *inch fresh ginger, chopped*
- 2 *cloves garlic, chopped*
- 1½ *teaspoons ground coriander seed*
- 1 *teaspoon ground cumin*
- ¼ *teaspoon turmeric*

Use this paste for hot curries.

• Grind all ingredients in a blender, adding a little water to the mixture to obtain a smooth paste.

HOMEMADE CHILI POWDER

• In a blender or grinder combine 4 pequín chilies and 3 ancho chilies (pages 27–29), 1½ tablespoons cuminseed, 1 teaspoon oregano, and 1 teaspoon garlic powder.

RED CHILI PASTE

- 8 *dried red chilies*
- *Boiling water to cover*
- ¼ *cup olive oil*
- 1 *clove garlic, peeled*
- *Coarse salt*
- 1 *cup boiling stock*

This paste can be used in recipes calling for fresh chilies. It will keep for 2–3 weeks refrigerated.

• Open chilies and remove seeds. Cover with boiling water and leave to soak for 2 hours. Drain. Combine in blender with oil, garlic, salt, and stock. Reduce to smooth purée.

MILD YELLOW CHILI PASTE

- *2 dozen yellow fresh chilies, blanched, rinsed under cold water, and seeded*
- *2 tablespoons peanut or vegetable oil*
- *2 tablespoons vinegar*
- *Coarse salt*

This paste can be used in recipes calling for a mild chili flavor. It will keep refrigerated for 2–3 weeks.

• Combine all ingredients in a blender and reduce to a smooth purée.

RAS EL HANOUT

- *½ tablespoon mace*
- *½ tablespoon allspice*
- *10 cardamom seeds, peeled*
- *1 whole nutmeg (or 1 tablespoon, ground)*
- *½ tablespoon laos root, page 24*
- *½ tablespoon black peppercorns*
- *½ tablespoon white peppercorns*
- *1 tablespoon dried gingerroot*
- *½ tablespoon ground cinnamon*
- *2 whole cloves*
- *1 teaspoon turmeric*
- *1 teaspoon aniseed*

This is a mixture of spices used in Moroccan dishes, particularly in tajines (Moroccan stews). In Moroccan markets variations of this mixture are sold already ground. Since many of the authentic ingredients are not available in the United States, I am giving here a simplified version which you can make yourself. Keep it in a tightly sealed jar. It is also delicious as a flavoring for non-Moroccan meat and vegetable dishes.

• Use a spice grinder to combine the spices.

SPICED PEPPER

• Use this with steaks, roasts, or grilled chicken. Combine 4 tablespoons coarsely ground pepper with 2 tablespoons thyme, 1 teaspoon garlic powder, 1 tablespoon Hungarian paprika, and 1 tablespoon caraway seeds.

ACHIOTE OIL

This oil is not hot, but it gives food the red orange color and subtle flavor characteristic of Caribbean and Latin American dishes. Achiote seeds (also called annatto seeds) are available in Latin American specialty stores and some supermarkets.

• Heat about a cup of peanut or vegetable oil in a saucepan and add about ¼ cup of achiote seeds. Cover, turn down the heat, and cook for a minute. Cool, strain, and keep the oil in a tightly sealed jar in the refrigerator. Use for frying meat or fish.

PIRI-PIRI (AFRICAN CHILI OIL)

• Heat a cup of olive, vegetable, or peanut oil and pour into a jar which contains 4 or 5 small fresh or dried red chilies. Seal tightly and keep for a month before using. Use for frying foods that would benefit from a subtle chili flavor, or for basting grilled meats and poultry.

SPICED VINEGAR

• In a saucepan combine one bottle white wine vinegar with a teaspoon each cloves, peppercorns, sugar, and a 1-inch piece of fresh ginger cut into slices. Add a tablespoon sugar, 2 dried chilies, and bring to boil, covered. Simmer for 2 minutes, remove from heat, and return to the bottle with the spices.

Use in salads and any other dishes calling for vinegar that might benefit from this spicy flavor.

KENYAN HOT PEPPER SHERRY

• Similar to a condiment used in the Caribbean, this keeps indefinitely and is used for flavoring soups and stews. Put 4 or 5 fresh hot chilies in a quart glass jar and fill it up with sherry. Let stand, tightly sealed and away from the light, for a month before using.

COCONUT MILK

• Coconut milk is not difficult to make and it is worth the time. It is used as a "stock" for many Indian, Caribbean, and Southeast Asian dishes and can be frozen. It keeps for up to a week in the refrigerator.

To buy coconuts, choose the heaviest ones and shake to see how much liquid there is inside. Don't buy coconuts with soft or wet "eyes." A 1½-pound coconut should yield about 3–4 cups water.

To open a coconut, puncture the eyes and pour the coconut water into a bowl. Heat the oven to 400 degrees and bake the coconut for 15 minutes. Remove it, put it on a hard surface, and split it with a hammer. The meat should come off easily (the heating is not necessary but it makes it easier).

You can now grate the coconut meat (peeling off the skin) or put it through a mincing machine. It can also be ground with water in a blender and the water then drained off.

Measure the amount of coconut and put equal amounts of *hot* water with the coconut into a blender. Blend until you have a thick liquid.

Sieve the liquid through a cheesecloth. The simplest way is to put it in a sieve and leave it over a bowl for a few hours. Press it down with a wooden spoon to squeeze out the remaining liquid and discard the pulp.

For a richer milk, let it stand and use only the top.

Desiccated coconut can be used with milk or water, but the resultant milk will be much thinner. Soak for an hour in hot water or milk using about ½ cup coconut to 1 cup liquid.

TAMARIND WATER

Tamarind is sold as a paste in Indian and Indonesian stores and is often used in preparing dishes from these countries. The paste keeps indefinitely and is well worth buying.

• To make the water, bring a cup of water to a boil. Pour it over a tablespoon of the paste and mix well.

GHEE

Ghee is clarified butter used in Indian cooking. When the butter is heated and kept simmering the milk solids separate from the fat. The solids are strained off carefully, leaving the clear fat which keeps for up to three months at room temperature. It is particularly useful for frying since it burns at a far higher temperature than butter and gives an interesting nutty flavor to the food.

• Melt 1 pound unsalted butter without browning it over a medium flame and bring it gently to the boil. Skim off the white foam which rises to the surface, reduce heat, and simmer gently, uncovered, for 45 minutes until the milk solids on the bottom are brown and the butter on top is clear and transparent.

Strain the butter through a sieve lined with 4 layers of cheesecloth. If it is not perfectly clear, strain again. Store in an airtight jar.

HOMEMADE YOGHURT

• Yoghurt is one of the simplest things to make. Having for years messed with yoghurt makers and expensive cultures I eventually discovered what seems to be the cheapest and easiest way to produce good homemade yoghurt. You simply take a spoonful of plain commercial yoghurt and add it to approximately a pint of warmed milk (if the milk is too hot you will kill the culture: put your finger in the milk, if you can keep it there and slowly count to ten without it burning it is cool enough) and put it in a thermos flask. Leave it for about 8 hours and your yoghurt should be done. It may need longer to set at the beginning. Each time you want to make more yoghurt, add a little of the last batch to warmed milk.

I bring the milk to a boil to kill any bacteria that may interfere with the yoghurt bacteria, and let it cool, covered so that a skin does not form.

For a thick yoghurt, powdered milk may be added.

You can use yoghurt in curries, stews, or sauces, in salad dressings, or serve it on its own as a cool accompaniment to spicy food.

Yoghurt can also be made by keeping the mixture warm on the back of the stove or in a warm oven (not hot or the bacteria will be destroyed). Yoghurt makers are really glorified hot plates. They keep the yoghurt warm at a constant temperature.

SOUP

This chapter is divided into hot and cold soups, some of which are substantial enough to constitute a main course. Do not overspice soup or use commercial curry powder. The individual spices should permeate the mixture. When the soup is made the day before, its flavor improves and becomes more pronounced.

Keep grated coconut and chopped almonds or peanuts on hand to garnish these soups. Dried vegetables should be washed and picked over before being cooked. Although it is not necessary to soak them in advance, doing so cuts down cooking time. Since any foam that accumulates tends to make the soup bitter, you should be careful to skim off any that rises to the surface.

Don't take shortcuts when you are preparing soup. You will only be disappointed by the results. It is very important to have a good stock. Bouillon cubes will not do the trick. Stocks can be made from leftover meat, chicken, fish, and vegetables, and then frozen until you need them. The following stocks are also good for gravies and stews.

CHICKEN OR MEAT STOCK

Chicken carcass or meat bones
Onion stuck with cloves
Chopped carrots
Chopped leek or celery, with leaves
Herb bouquet (parsley, thyme, bay leaf, tied in cheesecloth)
Giblets (necks, gizzards, etc.)
Bacon rind
Mushroom peelings
Whole peppercorns
Bay leaf
Fresh parsley sprigs
Coarse salt
Water to cover

• Break up any large bones and chop the vegetables. You can improve the stock if you fry them before adding them to the pot. Use a large, heavy casserole—do not use aluminum pans.

• Simmer gently for 3–4 hours, covered. Strain and refrigerate. The fat will rise to the top in a lump. Remove it and either freeze the stock for later use or store in refrigerator.

FISH STOCK

Fish bones, head, tail
Fresh sprigs dill or parsley (or both)
Bay leaf
Onion studded with cloves
1 *cup dry white wine*
Whole peppercorns (about 8)
Coarse salt
Water to cover

• Simmer gently, covered, for about 2 hours. Strain and refrigerate or freeze for later use.

JELLIED AVOCADO SOUP

2 *very ripe avocados*
2 *cans consommé madrilène* at room temperature
½ *teaspoon chili powder*
1 *tablespoon finely chopped onion or scallion*
Coarse salt and freshly ground pepper
Juice of half a lemon
About ½ cup sour cream
Cayenne pepper
Fresh chopped dill or chives to garnish

An extremely simple soup, it is good for entertaining. Steaks, chops, roasts may follow for dinner, or you might serve it for lunch with dark bread and butter, followed by eggs or cheese.

• Peel the avocados and mash them with a fork. Mix them thoroughly in a bowl with the consommé. Add the chili powder and onion, salt and pepper to taste, and mix in the lemon juice. Chill.

Put the jellied soup into individual serving bowls and put a tablespoon of sour cream on each serving. Sprinkle with Cayenne and the dill or chives. Serves 4–6.

COLD CURRIED SOUP

4 *tablespoons butter*
1 *large onion, diced*
2 *celery stalks with leaves, chopped*
1 *tablespoon Mild Curry Powder, page 40*
1 *tablespoon flour*
2 *apples, peeled and chopped*
About 1 cup cooked chicken meat, chopped
5 *cups chicken stock, page 49*
Juice of half a lemon
Coarse salt and freshly ground white pepper
1 *cup heavy cream*
Fresh chopped chives to garnish

• Melt the butter in a saucepan and gently cook the onion and celery without browning until soft. Add the curry powder and flour and cook for a couple of minutes, stirring.

Either combine the onion-curry mixture in a blender with the apples, chicken meat, and a cup of chicken broth or put it through a food mill with the apples and chicken. Return the purée to the saucepan and add the remaining broth, lemon juice, salt, and pepper. Bring to the boil, remove from heat, and chill overnight.

To serve, pour the soup into individual bowls, spoon the cream on top, and garnish with the chives. Serves 6.

CURRIED LENTIL SOUP

very good

- 2 *tablespoons butter or ghee page 45*
- 2 *onions, chopped*
- 2 *potatoes, diced*
- 1–1½ *tablespoons Mild Curry Powder, page 40*
- ½ *pound dried lentils*
- 4 *cups vegetable or chicken stock*
- *Juice of half a lemon*
- *Coarse salt and freshly ground pepper*
- *Fresh chopped parsley or mint to garnish*
- *Heavy cream (optional)*

This is a filling soup and needs only a salad such as Turkish Cucumbers in Yoghurt, page 168, and cheese to follow. Indian bread, page 157, or dark bread and unsalted butter are good with it. Homemade Chapattis, page 157, can be prepared while the soup is cooking.

• Heat the butter in a heavy casserole and sauté the onions and potatoes until golden. Add the curry powder and cook for a few minutes. Add the remaining ingredients (except parsley and cream) and simmer for an hour, skimming off any foam that may rise to the top. Put the mixture through a food mill (or purée in a blender) if you would like a smooth soup. Return to the casserole, bring to a boil, and serve. A little cream may be poured into each bowl of soup and the parsley sprinkled on top. Serves 4.

JAMAICAN RED PEA SOUP

- 1 *pound dried red beans*
- *Water to cover*
- 2 *onions, chopped*
- ¼ *pound salt pork*
- 4 *tablespoons chopped parsley*
- ½ *teaspoon thyme*
- 2 *celery stalks, with leaves*
- 2 *fresh chilies, chopped, pages 27–29*
- *Coarse salt and freshly ground pepper*

Red kidney beans can be used here. The ones used in Jamaica are smaller and similar to Mexican chili beans.

• Simmer the beans for 2½–3 hours with the remaining ingredients. Add more water, to cover, as they cook. Purée in a blender or put through the coarse blade of a food mill. Return to pan and correct seasoning. Serves 6.

CURRIED PEA SOUP

2 tablespoons butter
1 garlic clove, chopped
1 medium onion, chopped
1 tablespoon Mild Curry Powder, page 40
¾ pound shelled peas
1 lettuce, quartered
2 cups Chicken Stock, page 49
1 cup heavy cream
Juice of half a lemon
Coarse salt and freshly ground pepper
Fresh chopped chives, mint, basil, to garnish

When fresh peas are in season this is an excellent way to use the large peas that appear on the market. After it, grilled fish or chicken, lamb chops, kidneys, or liver would be good as a main course.

• Melt the butter in a saucepan and soften the onion and the garlic without browning. Add the curry powder and cook for 2 minutes. Add the peas, lettuce, and 1 cup of chicken stock. Bring to a boil, reduce heat, and simmer for 15 minutes. Purée in a blender or sieve the mixture.

Return the mixture to the saucepan and add the remaining stock. Simmer for 5 minutes. Off heat, add the cream, lemon juice, and salt and pepper to taste. Chill.

To serve, pour the soup into individual bowls and garnish with a tablespoon of extra cream if you like, and the chopped herbs. Serves 4–6.

BLACK BEAN SOUP

1 pound black beans
Water to cover, plus about 4 cups
1 onion, coarsely chopped
1 carrot, sliced
3 celery stalks, including leaves, coarsely chopped
Herb bouquet (parsley, thyme, bay leaf, tied in cheesecloth)
4 whole allspice
2 cloves
¼ teaspoon mace
¼ teaspoon cinnamon
2 cloves garlic, chopped
1 fresh green chili, chopped, pages 27–29
Coarse salt and freshly ground pepper
¼ cup rum
Lemon slices
Sour cream

• Soak the beans overnight. Simmer in water with vegetables and herbs for about 3 hours, adding water if necessary. Stir in the rum, bring to boil, pour into heated soup bowls. In each bowl put a spoonful of sour cream and a slice of lemon. Serves 8.

HUNGARIAN ONION SOUP

- 4 *large onions*
- 3 *tablespoons butter*
- 2 *teaspoons Hungarian paprika*
- 6 *cups chicken or beef stock, homemade*
- 2 *tomatoes, peeled and chopped, page 34*
- ½ *teaspoon oregano*
- *Coarse salt and freshly ground black pepper*

A good stock is essential for this soup. Serve it with black bread.

• Slice the onions and soften them in the butter in a large, heavy saucepan. Sprinkle with paprika and cook for 2 minutes. Add the remaining ingredients and simmer gently for an hour. Correct seasoning and serve. Serves 6.

SPICY TOMATO SOUP

- 1 *medium onion, chopped*
- 2 *tablespoons butter*
- 1 *clove garlic, minced*
- 2 *green bell peppers, chopped*
- 1 *tablespoon flour*
- 1½ *pounds tomatoes, peeled and chopped, page 34*
- 4 *cups chicken or vegetable stock*
- ½ *teaspoon crushed coriander seed*
- ½ *teaspoon Tabasco sauce*
- ¼ *teaspoon Worcestershire sauce*
- 3 *teaspoons fresh grated horse-radish*
- *Dash tarragon vinegar to taste*
- *Coarse salt and freshly ground pepper*
- *Fresh chopped parsley or basil to garnish*
- *Croutons to garnish*

• Soften the onion in the butter with the garlic and peppers in a large, heavy-bottomed saucepan. Add the flour and cook for 2 minutes without burning. Add the remaining ingredients (except garnishes) and simmer gently for about 1½ hours. Correct seasoning, sprinkle on parsley or basil and croutons, and serve hot. Serves 4.

CHICKEN SOUP WITH RICE

1 3–4 *pound chicken*
Water to cover
Coarse salt
Freshly ground black pepper
1 *tablespoon peanut or vegetable oil*
1 *medium onion, chopped*
½ *inch fresh ginger, chopped*
2 *tablespoons Macadamia nuts, chopped*
1 *teaspoon turmeric*

Garnishes
Rice, page 153
Chopped or sliced hardboiled eggs
Shredded cabbage
Potato chips, crushed
Chopped celery
Slices of lemon

Sambal
4 *tablespoons chopped fresh or canned chilies, pages* 27–29
2 *tablespoons chopped fresh ginger*
1 *tablespoon vinegar*
Chicken broth to moisten as needed

The soup itself is not hot but the sambal which goes with it as a relish is. This is more of a stew than a soup and certainly constitutes a main course. A salad to follow would be plenty. It is also an attractive dish for entertaining, the garnishes can be arranged on a plate or in little bowls and add color to the table.

• Simmer the chicken in water to cover with salt and pepper until it is done. Remove, cool slightly, and bone. Meanwhile fry the onion, ginger, and Macadamia nuts in the oil and add with the turmeric to the simmering broth.

Return the boned chicken to the soup, bring to a boil, remove from heat, and serve with the garnishes and sambal, to which people help themselves at the table. The sambal is made by combining the chilies, ginger, vinegar, and adding enough chicken broth to make it fairly liquid. Serves 4–6.

HOT AND SOUR SOUP

4 *dried black Chinese mushrooms*
¼ *pound lean pork*
2 *bean curd cakes*
4 *cups beef or chicken stock*
2 *tablespoons dry sherry*
2 *tablespoons vinegar*
1 *teaspoon soy sauce*
½ *teaspoon Tabasco sauce*
Coarse salt and freshly ground pepper
2 *tablespoons cornstarch mixed to a paste with* 2 *tablespoons cold water*
1 *egg, beaten*
About 1 *tablespoon sesame oil*
1 *scallion, chopped*

After this Chinese soup you may want to continue with a Chinese meal. Twice-cooked Szechwan Pork, page 121, or Chicken in Chili-Walnut Sauce, page 103, served with rice and Chinese-style vegetables would follow very well.

If you have leftovers to use up, thinly sliced cooked pork, beef, duck, chicken, or shrimp can be successfully used. Add them at the end so that they heat through without becoming overcooked.

• Soak the mushrooms in water for half an hour. Drain, reserving the liquid, and slice into thin strips. Slice the pork and the bean curd in strips. Bring the stock to the boil and simmer the pork and mushrooms for 10 minutes. Add the bean curd and simmer for a couple more minutes. Add the sherry, vinegar, soy sauce, salt, pepper, and cornstarch mixture. Simmer for a few minutes until thick. Off heat add the egg, stirring constantly. Add the oil and scallion, mix in, and serve. Serves 4.

SHRIMP AND VEGETABLE SOUP

1 *medium onion, chopped*
1 *clove garlic, chopped*
2 *chilies, fresh or canned, minced*
2 *tablespoons peanut, vegetable, or coconut oil*
1 *teaspoon coriander, ground*
4 *cups Coconut Milk, page 44*
1 *pound diced vegetables (sweet corn, french beans, peanuts, zucchini, eggplant, etc.)*
½ *pound peeled shrimp*
1 *teaspoon grated lemon rind*
Coarse salt
Freshly ground pepper

Follow this Southeast Asian soup with grilled meat or chicken served with rice. Be careful not to overcook the shrimp. Three or four minutes is plenty, and remember that it will go on cooking even after the soup has left the stove.

• Fry the onion, garlic, and chilies in the oil until golden. Add the coriander and fry for 2 minutes, stirring. Add the coconut milk and the vegetables and simmer, covered, until vegetables are just tender. Add the shrimp, lemon rind, salt, and pepper and cook for a few minutes—just enough barely to cook the shrimp. Serve hot. Serves 4.

INDONESIAN VEGETABLE SOUP

- 2 *medium onions, chopped*
- 1 *clove garlic, chopped*
- ½ *teaspoon turmeric*
- 1 *teaspoon coriander, ground*
- ½ *teaspoon chili powder*
- 2 *tablespoons peanut or vegetable oil*
- 1 *lemon grass stalk (if available) or 1 teaspoon powdered sereh, page 24*
- 4 *cups* Coconut Milk, *page 44*
- 1 *pound diced raw vegetables (string beans, Brussels sprouts, cabbage, carrots, peas, potatoes, etc.)*
- *Coarse salt and freshly ground pepper*
- 1 *teaspoon grated lemon rind*

This soup is substantial enough for a main lunch course. For an evening meal, serve something fairly light and plain after it.

• Combine the onions, garlic, turmeric, coriander, chili powder, and oil in an electric blender and purée. Fry the mixture in a large saucepan for about 3–4 minutes, stirring constantly. Add the remaining ingredients and simmer gently, covered, for about 20 minutes, or until vegetables are cooked. Serve hot, garnished with grated coconut and chopped fried onion, if you like. Serves 4.

HORS D'OEUVRES

Some of the hors d'oeuvres in this chapter are suitable for handing around with drinks before dinner; others are good as first-course dishes or lunch entrées. Hot, spicy hors d'oeuvres are particularly good in the summer with long drinks. Many of the dishes in this chapter—tacos, anticuchos, spareribs, satés, for example—are delicious cooked outside over charcoal and served with dips and sauces on the side.

Marinated raw fish dishes from Latin America and the Caribbean are excellent light starters to an evening meal and can be made in advance.

CHILI CASHEWS

1 *pound plain cashews*
2 *tablespoons peanut oil*
1 *teaspoon chili powder*
¼ *teaspoon ground chilies*

• Fry the nuts in the peanut oil until golden brown. Sprinkle with the chili powder and ground chilies while hot. Season with coarse salt.

CURRIED STUFFED EGGS

6 *hardboiled eggs*
3 *tablespoons Mayonnaise, page 181 (or commercial mayonnaise can be used)*
3 *or* 4 *scallions, chopped*
About ½ cup chopped shrimp, tuna, peppers, or what you will
Coarse salt to taste
1 *tablespoon Mild Curry Powder, page 40*
Paprika

If you have leftover meat, chicken, or fish, vegetables and so on, they can be chopped and added to the yolk mixture.

• Cut the eggs in half and remove the yolks. Mash the yolks in a bowl with the remaining ingredients except the paprika, adding more mayonnaise as needed to obtain the right consistency. Fill the whites with the mixture, sprinkle with paprika, and arrange on a serving plate.

DEVILLED NUTS

Almonds are the best prepared this way but skinned filberts, peanuts, and walnuts are also very good. Serve very hot.

• Pour boiling water over almonds and peel them. Fry them lightly in butter or oil (use a nut or vegetable oil, not olive oil) until they are golden brown. Drain them on paper and sprinkle them liberally with coarse salt and Cayenne pepper.

CHEESE STRAWS (GREAT BRITAIN)

- 1½ *cups white flour*
- *Coarse salt*
- ¼ *teaspoon Hungarian paprika*
- ½ *teaspoon Cayenne pepper*
- 12 *tablespoons butter*
- 1½ *cups grated Parmesan and Cheddar cheese (mixed)*
- ¼ *teaspoon Tabasco*
- 1 *egg yolk*

• Sift the flour and add the salt, paprika, and Cayenne. Rub in the butter until the mixture is like oatmeal. Add the cheese, Tabasco, and egg yolk. Make into a smooth dough, adding water as necessary. Roll out onto a floured board and cut in narrow strips, about ¼ inch wide and 3 inches long. Bake in preheated oven at 400 degrees for about 7–8 minutes, or until golden.

JAMAICAN PLANTAIN CHIPS

- *Plantains*
- *Oil for deep-frying*
- *Coarse salt*

Serve these with drinks or with spicy grilled meat. Use plantains that are green or half-ripe.

• Slice the peeled plantains into rounds. Heat the oil until it registers 375 degrees on a frying thermometer. Fry the plantains until crisp. Drain on paper towels.

MOROCCAN CARROTS

- 1 *pound carrots, peeled and cut in quarters*
- *Water to cover*
- 4 *tablespoons olive oil*
- 1 *tablespoon vinegar or lemon juice*
- *Coarse salt and freshly ground pepper*
- ½ *teaspoon cuminseed*
- 1 *teaspoon Cayenne*
- 2 *tablespoons fresh chopped parsley to garnish*

Flat Arabian bread (pita) goes with this hors d'oeuvre. Tahina (sesame paste) and Greek feta cheese are also available at Arab specialty shops and make a good opening spread. Afterward, perhaps roast or grilled lamb, or kebabs and a green vegetable.

• Simmer the carrots in water until barely tender. Remove and coat with the olive oil mixed with the vinegar. Season with salt, pepper, cumin, and Cayenne. Sprinkle with parsley and serve when cool.

MOROCCAN-STYLE OLIVES

½ pound green olives
Juice of 2 lemons
2 cloves garlic, minced
1 tablespoon paprika
¼ teaspoon ground chili
½ teaspoon cumin
2 tablespoons olive oil
½ cup chopped fresh parsley
Coarse salt to taste

Use cracked green olives. These are unripe olives, cracked and soaked in brine. Those available in the United States should be washed, drained, and boiled before being marinated.

• Put the olives in an earthenware dish, combine the remaining ingredients, and pour onto the olives. Let stand overnight before serving.

ALBONDIGUITAS (LITTLE MEXICAN MEATBALLS)

1 tablespoon peanut oil or butter
1 medium onion, finely chopped
2 slices white homemade-type bread
Milk
1 pound ground beef
½ pound ground pork
2 eggs
1 tablespoon chili powder
Coarse salt and freshly ground pepper
2 tablespoons minced fresh parsley or coriander
Oil for frying

Serve these with toothpicks and a Mexican sauce (see sauce chapter for ideas).

• Heat the oil and cook the onion until soft but not browned. Meanwhile soak the bread in the milk.

In a large bowl combine the meat, eggs, onion, bread, chili powder, salt, pepper, and parsley. Form into bite-size balls.

Heat the oil in a skillet and fry the balls until browned and cooked through. Drain and serve hot. Makes about 30.

Note: Another way to cook these is in a stock made from meat and tomato juice. Simmer them with enough liquid to cover for about 45 minutes. Drain and reserve the stock for other uses.

MUSHROOMS PAPRIKASH

- 3 *tablespoons butter*
- 2 *tablespoons chopped shallots*
- 1 *pound mushrooms, sliced*
- *Coarse salt and freshly ground pepper*
- 2 *teaspoons Hungarian paprika*
- 1 *teaspoon flour*
- ½ *cup sour cream*
- *Fresh chopped parsley to garnish*

This Hungarian hors d'oeuvre is delicious on toast or served in little pastry shells which have been filled and heated through in the oven.

• Melt the butter in a large frying pan and soften the shallots without burning. Add the mushrooms and salt and cook for about 10 minutes, or until the juices begin to form. Add the pepper, paprika, and flour and cook for another 2 minutes, stirring. Add the cream just long enough to heat through, remove, and serve with chopped parsley on top. Serves 4.

MARINATED SPICY BEEF STRIPS

- 1 *pound lean steak (any cut)*
- 1 *clove garlic, chopped*
- 1 *medium onion, chopped*
- 2 *tablespoons finely chopped fresh ginger*
- 1 *teaspoon crushed red chili peppers*
- 2 *teaspoons soy sauce*
- ¼ *cup peanut or vegetable oil*
- *Dash Tabasco sauce*

Sauce

- 2 *tablespoons sugar*
- ½ *cup red wine vinegar*
- 3 *tablespoons plum jam*
- 2 *tablespoons mango chutney*
- *Dash Worcestershire sauce*
- *Coarse salt and freshly ground pepper*

Marinate the beef overnight. Serve the strips with toothpicks, with the sauce in a separate bowl as a dip.

• Cut the meat against the grain into thin strips about 2½ inches long, ½ inch wide. Put in a bowl with the marinating ingredients and marinate overnight. Combine the ingredients for the sauce and set aside.

Heat 1 tablespoon oil in a skillet and add the meat. Stir-fry over high heat for about 2 minutes. Do not overcook or the meat will curl and toughen.

Pour any juices into the sauce, mix, and serve.

TACOS

Tacos are tortillas, usually fried, wrapped around chopped meat, sometimes folded and secured with a toothpick, sometimes simply folded over. They lend themselves to a variety of fillings: chopped meat, mashed beans, diced chicken or fish, cheese, chopped lettuce, chopped tomato, etc. For a party you can arrange bowls of Mexican sauces (see index) on the table, Mexican Black Beans, Guacamole, page 66, chopped meat, fresh and canned chilies, chopped onion, and a plate of hot tortillas—all to be eaten with the fingers.

Tacos are also good in a complete Mexican meal which might include a meat or chicken dish (see index), Enchiladas, page 149, Mexican Beans, page 151, Fried Plantains, page 141, Mexican Refried Beans, page 150, and rice.

Fillings:

1. *Cheese Tacos:* Fill with slices of Monterey Jack (or similar cheese), diced jalapeño chilies, pages 27–29, chopped tomatoes, salt, and pepper.

2. *Ham Taco:* Fill with diced ham which you have mixed with diced onion, cream cheese, and chopped jalapeño or serrano chilies, pages 27–29.

3. *Sweet Pepper Tacos:* Soften chopped bell peppers and onions in oil, add some peeled tomatoes, a little sour cream, salt, and pepper, and heat through.

4. *Chorizo Tacos:* Fill with chopped, skinned, fried chorizos which you have mixed with equal amount of diced cheese (Monterey Jack or similar).

5. *Bean Tacos:* Fill with leftover Mexican Refried Beans, page 150, and cheese, with diced jalapeño chili.

6. *Picadillo Tacos:* Fill with leftover Picadillo, page 111, or make the recipe using half the quantity.

• To cook tacos heat olive oil in a large heavy-bottomed skillet and fry, turning once, until golden. Drain on paper towels and serve hot.

CALIFORNIA TACOS

Tortillas
Chopped lettuce
Chopped chilies
Chopped onions
Grated Cheddar
Chopped tomatoes
Coarse salt
Freshly ground pepper

A light snack, an hors d'oeuvre, or a party dish, tacos are simple to make and can be prepared (except for the final frying) in advance. Use quantities according to how many people you are feeding.

• Fry the tortillas in a light oil, fill them with the vegetables and cheese, season with salt and pepper, and fold one side of the tortilla over to form a kind of sandwich. Serve hot.

PANUCHOS

12 *4-inch tortillas*
Lard or peanut oil
½ *recipe for Mexican Beans, page 151, or (Mexican Refried Beans, page 150)*
3 *hardboiled eggs, sliced*
2 *whole cooked chicken breasts, boned and diced*
Grated fresh Parmesan or Cheddar cheese
Yucatán Hot Pepper Sauce, page 179

These miniature tortilla snacks originate in Yucatán. They are simple to make and are good as an appetizer or light lunch dish.

• Make a slit in each tortilla and fill the pocket with the beans and a slice of egg. Fry in the lard or oil. Drain on paper towels. Serve topped with chicken and cheese, the sauce spooned on top.

CHILIES STUFFED WITH CREAM CHEESE

Small canned or fresh red or green chili peppers, pages 27–29
Cream cheese
Coarse salt
Chopped nuts

Stuffed and sliced thinly, these fiery little peppers are delicious on rounds of dark bread or crackers.

• Remove the veins and the seeds from the chilies.

Mash the cheese with the salt and nuts and stuff the mixture into the chilies. Refrigerate for a few hours.

Slice the chilies very thinly with a sharp knife and place on buttered bread or crackers.

HUNGARIAN CREAM CHEESE DIP

- 1 *8-ounce package cream cheese*
- ½ *cup sour cream*
- 4 *tablespoons butter at room temperature*
- 1 *teaspoon Dijon-type mustard*
- 4 *teaspoons caraway seeds*
- *Coarse salt*
- 2 *tablespoons Hungarian paprika*
- *Chopped chives to garnish*

Raw vegetables such as cauliflower, carrots, broccoli, celery, and cherry tomatoes are delicious dipped into this mixture. Arrange the vegetables around a plate with the cream cheese in the center. Dark bread and crackers are also good with it.

• Mash the cheese in a bowl with the remaining ingredients except the chives. Put the mixture into a clean bowl and sprinkle with the chives.

LIPTAUER KÄSE

- 1 *cup cottage cheese*
- 1 *stick butter, at room temperature*
- 2 *anchovies, drained and finely chopped*
- 1 *tablespoon capers, chopped*
- 1 *tablespoon caraway seeds*
- 1 *tablespoon chives, chopped*
- 1 *tablespoon dry mustard*
- 1 *tablespoon Hungarian paprika*
- ½ *teaspoon celery salt*

This can be served in a mound, sprinkled with paprika, so that guests help themselves and spread the mixture on black or rye bread, or it can be used as a spread for canapés.

• Mash all the ingredients together and shape into a mound. Sprinkle with extra paprika. Will keep for several days in the refrigerator.

WELSH RAREBIT

- ½ *pound aged Cheddar*
- 1 *tablespoon butter*
- ½ *cup brown ale*
- *Coarse salt and freshly ground pepper*
- ½ *teaspoon Dijon-type mustard*
- *Cayenne pepper to taste*

Cheddar cheese and Cayenne pepper are very good together. Rarebit is best made with a good dry aged Cheddar, brown ale, and spiced with Cayenne and hot mustard.

For a party, Welsh rarebit can be served like a Swiss fondue—but much more economically since beer is cheaper than kirsch and cheddar is cheaper than Gruyère. Pour the mixture into a chafing dish and keep it in the middle of the table (don't let it get too hot). Your guests can either dip pieces of hot toast on the end of a fork into the mixture or it can be poured onto the toast on their plate. Beer is, of course, the drink to have with it.

• Slice or coarsely grate the cheese. Melt it over low heat and add the remaining ingredients, stirring constantly until you have a smooth paste. Serve at once. Serves 4.

DEVILLED SARDINE CANAPÉS

• Mash the contents of 2 cans of sardines with the juice of a lemon, a few drops of Tabasco sauce, 1 teaspoon Dijon-type mustard, ½ teaspoon Cayenne pepper, salt, and freshly ground black pepper. Spread the mixture on buttered toast fingers and place under a broiler until sizzling. Serve hot. Makes about 12.

CURRIED ANCHOVY CANAPÉS

• Mash the contents of 2 cans of anchovies with 2 tablespoons softened butter, 2 tablespoons blue cheese, and 1 tablespoon of curry powder. Spread buttered toast fingers with a little chutney and then with the anchovy mixture. Makes about 12.

GUACAMOLE

3 *ripe avocados*
3 *tomatoes, peeled and chopped, page 34*
¼–½ *teaspoon chili powder*
½ *small onion, minced*
2 *tablespoons fresh coriander, chopped*
Coarse salt and freshly ground pepper
Dash kirsch (optional)
Lemon juice

Serve as an hors d'oeuvre with corn chips or as a salad with Mexican food.

• Peel, pit, and mash the avocados. Combine with the tomatoes in a bowl. Add the chili powder, onion, coriander, and kirsch if you like. Season with salt and pepper and squeeze lemon over the top to prevent turning brown. Decorate with a sprig of coriander in center.

PERUVIAN CEVICHE

- 2 *pounds raw fish (sole, red snapper, or any white-fleshed fish)*
- 3–4 *hot red or green chilies, pages 27–29*
- 1 *cup lime juice*
- 1 *cup lemon juice*
- *Coarse salt and freshly ground pepper*
- *Fresh chopped coriander (Chinese parsley)*
- 1 *medium onion, cut in rings*

For this popular Peruvian hors d'oeuvre, raw fish is marinated in lime and lemon juice which turns it white and "cooks" it. Serve the fish on oiled lettuce leaves.

• Bone the fish and cut it into 2-inch pieces. Chop the chilies finely and put in a bowl with the lime and lemon juice. Add the fish, season, and mix thoroughly. Leave for several hours, or overnight if possible. To serve, sprinkle with coriander and serve on lettuce garnished with onion rings. Serves 6–8 as an appetizer.

CEVICHE SALAD

- 2 *pounds raw fish (see above)*
- 1 *medium onion, chopped*
- 3–4 *hot red or green chilies, chopped*
- 1 *clove garlic, chopped*
- 1 *cup lime juice*
- 1 *cup lemon juice*
- *Coarse salt and freshly ground black pepper*
- 1 *red bell pepper*
- 1 *green bell pepper*
- 1 *tomato, peeled, seeded, and chopped*

An expanded version of ceviche, this contains tomatoes and peppers. Serve it on oiled lettuce leaves with slices of avocado sprinkled with lemon juice and Spanish onion rings if you like.

• Bone the fish and cut it into 2-inch pieces. Combine it in a bowl with the onion, chilies, garlic, lime juice, and lemon juice. Season and leave to marinate for a few hours or overnight.

Slice the peppers and add to the fish with the tomato. Toss and arrange on lettuce. Serves 8 as an appetizer.

Note: You can vary this salad by adding chopped capers, chopped parsley, coriander leaves, or a dash of Tabasco sauce.

SCALLOP CEVICHE

- 1 *pound raw bay scallops*
- 1 *cup fresh lime juice*
- 1 *small onion, chopped*
- 2 *green chilies, chopped*
- 2 *tablespoons chopped fresh parsley*
- ½ *cup olive oil*
- *Coarse salt and freshly ground white pepper*

• Cut the scallops into quarters and cover with the lime juice. Marinate overnight. Add the remaining ingredients. Serve with toothpicks as an hors d'oeuvre, or as an appetizer with dark bread or tortillas. Serves 4.

DEVILLED SOFT ROES

½ pound soft roes
Flour for dredging
Coarse salt and freshly ground pepper
Cayenne pepper
Dry mustard
2 tablespoons butter
Lemon juice
Toast

A British dish, this is good either as an hors d'oeuvre or as a light lunch. In Britain it is often served at the end of a meal as a savory.

• Dredge the roes in flour which you have highly seasoned with salt, pepper, Cayenne, and mustard. Heat the butter and fry the roes on either side. Squeeze on plenty of lemon juice and serve on buttered toast. Serves 4 as an hors d'oeuvre.

MARINATED CHILI SHRIMP

¾ cup olive oil
⅓ cup vinegar
Juice of a lemon
1 teaspoon prepared horseradish
2 tablespoons prepared Dijon-type mustard
1 teaspoon chili powder
Coarse salt and freshly ground pepper
1 tablespoon tomato purée
1 pound peeled shrimp, barely cooked or raw
1 Spanish onion, sliced into thin rings
Fresh chopped coriander to garnish (parsley may be substituted if coriander is unavailable)

Raw, peeled shrimp can be used here. The vinegar and lemon juice "cook" the shrimp when it is left in the marinade overnight. If you prefer, cook the shrimp first but only for 3 minutes or less. If overcooked, the shrimp will become woolly and tasteless.

Tortillas are good with this Mexican recipe.

• Combine all ingredients except shrimp, onion, and coriander. Toss the shrimp thoroughly in the mixture and leave for 8 hours or overnight. Arrange on a serving dish and place the onion rings on top. Garnish with coriander and serve. Serves 4.

CREOLE SHRIMP

- 1 *pound shrimp, cooked and peeled*
- ½ *cup olive oil*
- 1 *tablespoon vinegar*
- 2 *scallions, chopped*
- 2 *tablespoons Red Chili Sauce, page 178 (or bottled)*
- 1 *tablespoon Creole mustard*
- *Coarse salt and freshly ground pepper*
- 1 *tablespoon fresh chopped parsley*

Serve this shrimp with thin slices of toast. It is an excellent dish for entertaining.

• Marinate the shrimp overnight in a mixture of the remaining ingredients. Serves 4 as an appetizer.

SHRIMP REMOULADE

- 1 *pound shrimp, cooked and peeled*
- 1 *cup Mayonnaise, page 181*
- 3 *teaspoons Dijon-type mustard*
- 1 *tablespoon chopped capers*
- 1 *tablespoon chopped gherkins*
- 1 *tablespoon chopped fresh tarragon (or 1 teaspoon dried)*
- 1 *tablespoon chopped fresh parsley*
- ½ *teaspoon anchovy paste*
- *Coarse salt and freshly ground pepper*

Serve this on or with thin slices of toast.

• Marinate the shrimp for 1 or 2 hours in a mixture of the remaining ingredients. Serves 4 as an appetizer.

DEVILLED CRAB AU GRATIN

- 4 *cooked crabs*
- 1 *tablespoon butter, melted*
- 2 *tablespoons fresh white breadcrumbs*
- 1 *tablespoon freshly grated Parmesan cheese*
- ½ *cup heavy cream*
- *Worcestershire sauce*
- *Dash Tabasco sauce*
- ½ *teaspoon Dijon-type mustard*
- *Dash Cayenne*
- *Coarse salt and freshly ground pepper*

You can also serve this as a main dish, followed by a salad.

• Put the crabmeat in a bowl with the remaining ingredients. Mix thoroughly, put the mixture into the crab shells, dot with extra butter, and dust with extra Parmesan and Cayenne. Bake in a preheated 375-degree oven for about 15 minutes. Serves 4.

SCANDINAVIAN MUSTARD HERRING

- 4 *herring, sliced*
- 2 *tablespoons Dijon-type mustard*
- ½ *cup olive oil*
- ½ *cup heavy cream*
- 1 *tablespoon brown sugar*
- 1 *tablespoon vinegar*
- 3 *tablespoons diced pickle or capers*
- *Coarse salt and freshly ground white pepper*
- 1 *tablespoon fresh chopped chives*

You may use salted herring which has been soaked or herring marinated in vinegar and sold in jars. This dish is great for lunch with hardboiled egg slices and new potatoes, or served on black or rye bread like a Danish open sandwich. To serve it as an hors d'oeuvre, I suggest you accompany it with slices of fresh black bread and unsalted butter.

• Arrange the herring on a serving platter. Combine the mustard, oil, cream, sugar, vinegar, pickles, salt, and pepper. Pour over the herring and sprinkle with chives. Serves 4.

CRABES FARCIS (GUADELOUPE)

- 6 *crabs*
- 1 *chili pepper, minced, pages 27–29*
- 3 *tablespoons chopped fresh parsley*
- 3 *tablespoons chopped fresh chives*
- 2 *cloves garlic, minced*
- 1 *tablespoon lime juice*
- 1½ *cups fresh breadcrumbs*
- *Coarse salt and freshly ground pepper*
- ¼ *teaspoon ground allspice*
- 3 *tablespoons dark rum*
- *Butter*
- *Cayenne pepper*

This works very well with fresh lump crabmeat. Arrange the mixture in scallop shells in the manner of Coquilles St. Jacques.

• Cook the crabs in boiling water for 8–10 minutes. Cool. Remove the meat from the shells and claws and chop. Scrub the shells and set aside.

Combine the chili pepper, herbs, garlic, lime juice, 1 cup breadcrumbs, and crabmeat in a mixing bowl. Season and add the allspice and rum. Mix thoroughly. Sprinkle with remaining breadcrumbs, Cayenne pepper, dot with butter, and bake in a 375-degree oven until lightly browned. Serves 6 as an hors d'oeuvre.

INDONESIAN SATÉ

• Saté is a little kebab. It can be served either as an hors d'oeuvre or a main course. Beef, lamb, pork, kidneys, liver, fish, or chicken are cut in ¾-inch cubes, marinated, and threaded on small wooden skewers. They are then broiled over charcoal and served with a variety of sauces, most of them piquant. The skewers should be soaked in water before they are used or they will burn.

Satés can also be served accompanied by rice, various sambals, page 190, chutneys, pages 188–189, and slices of orange.

See the index under Saté for the different kinds which are listed in the meat, fish, and poultry sections of this book. See under Saté Sauces and Saté Relishes for suggestions.

ANTICUCHOS

These little beef-heart kebabs are sold like hotdogs in the streets of Peru. They are marinated in a mixture of spices and grilled over charcoal after being threaded on tiny cane skewers. You may also use liver, kidneys, beef, chicken, or seafood. One of the advantages of using beef heart (quite apart from its flavor) is that it is very cheap and goes a long way.

1 *beef heart*

Marinade

1 *cup red wine vinegar*
2 *cloves garlic, chopped*
1 *tablespoon cumin*
2 *fresh red chilies, diced, pages 27–29*
Coarse salt and freshly ground pepper

2 *dried chilies*
1 *tablespoon achiote seeds*
½ *cup olive oil*

• Trim the filaments from the beef heart and cut it into 1-inch cubes. Combine the marinade ingredients and marinate the beef in this mixture overnight.

Soak the chilies, torn into small pieces, in boiling water to cover for half an hour. Put the achiote seeds in a blender and grind to a powder (or use a pestle and mortar). Add the chilies with their liquid and the oil. Blend.

Cook the beef pieces, threaded on skewers, over charcoal or under a broiler. Combine ¾ of the marinade with the achiote mixture and baste the beef hearts with this as they are cooking. Serve immediately when cooked according to taste (I prefer them pink in the middle).

Note: Achiote seeds are red, irregularly shaped little seeds that can be bought in Latin American specialty stores and some supermarkets.

MEXICAN SPARERIBS

2 pounds pork ribs
Juice of a lemon
Coarse salt and freshly ground pepper
2 cloves garlic, sliced
1 medium onion, chopped
3 tomatoes, chopped
1 teaspoon sugar
2 teaspoons chili powder
Water as needed

In Mexico, pork ribs have much less fat than American ones. You will probably find the juices too greasy to scrape up into a sauce. See the chapter on sauces for a dipping sauce. The ribs can be served on a plate with the dipping sauce in the middle, and eaten with your fingers.

• Trim excess fat off the ribs and squeeze the lemon over them. Season them and place them in a roasting pan with the garlic and onion. Add the tomatoes and sprinkle the ribs with sugar and chili powder. Pour in enough water to cover the bottom of the pan and bake the ribs at 350 degrees in a preheated oven for about 1½ hours, or until crisp. Baste frequently with the sauce, adding more water if it dries up. Serves 4–6 as an hors d'oeuvre.

EGGS

The best breakfast I ever had was in Yucatán. Before the day heated up we headed for a café which overlooked the harbor. As we watched the boats come in, we would eat fried eggs served on black beans and fresh tortillas, surrounded by peas sprinkled with cheese and accompanied by a hot tomato-chili sauce. The eggs were not the anemic productions unworthy of their name, with shells like paper, that have taken over the American market today. They were free-range eggs with bright orange yolks.

Since there is no pleasure in a plain boiled "chicken-factory" egg, spices have come to play a very important role in the art of egg cookery. This chapter features dishes that are acceptable for breakfast, lunch, or dinner. Don't, however, substitute commercial curry powder or skimp on ingredients.

MEXICAN SCRAMBLED EGGS

- 8 *eggs*
- 2 *tablespoons heavy cream*
- *Coarse salt and freshly ground pepper*
- 2 *tablespoons butter*
- 1 *small onion, chopped*
- ½ *red or green bell pepper, chopped*
- 1 *tomato, peeled and chopped*
- 1 *tablespoon chili powder*
- 1 *tablespoon fresh chopped coriander*

Cook the eggs extremely slowly over very low heat, stirring constantly.

• Beat the eggs with the cream and season them with salt and pepper. Melt the butter in a heavy-bottomed pan and gently soften the onion with the pepper. Add tomato and the chili powder, cook for 2 minutes, then add the eggs, turning the heat down as low as it will go. Do not overcook the eggs; they should be slightly runny when you take them off the flame. Sprinkle with coriander. Serves 4.

YUCATÁN EGGS

- 6 *tablespoons peanut oil or lard*
- 8 *tortillas*
- ½ *recipe Mexican Beans, page* 151
- 8 *eggs*
- ½ *recipe Mexican Tomato Sauce, page* 178
- 2 *cups cooked green peas*
- 4 *tablespoons grated Parmesan or Cheddar cheese*
- *Bottled hot chili sauce to taste*
- *Coarse salt and freshly ground pepper*

• Heat the oil in a large skillet and fry the tortillas. Spread them with a layer of hot beans and keep warm. Fry the eggs and place an egg on top of each tortilla. Spoon the tomato sauce over the eggs and arrange the peas around them. Sprinkle with cheese, correct seasoning, and sprinkle on chili sauce. Serves 4 (2 each).

FLAMENCA EGGS

- 4 *chorizos*
- 2 *green bell peppers, chopped*
- 5 *tomatoes, peeled and chopped*
- *Butter*
- 8 *slices ham*
- 1 *pound peas, cooked*
- *Coarse salt and freshly ground pepper*

This Spanish dish can be made in individual ramekins or in a large casserole. Using 1 egg per person, it makes a pretty hors d'oeuvre served in the individual casseroles. For a main course, a large dish with 2 eggs per person is simpler.

Chorizos can be bought in Spanish or Mexican specialty stores or homemade. Italian hot pepper sausage is a good substitute.

• Slice the sausages thinly and fry with the peppers. Add the tomatoes and cook for 3 minutes. Season and set aside.

In a buttered dish arrange a layer of ham, peas, and tomato mixture. Make a little indentation for each egg and break in the eggs. Finish with a little more tomato sauce and bake in a moderate oven until the eggs are set. Serves 4 as a main course.

HUEVOS RANCHEROS

- 5 *tablespoons lard or peanut oil*
- 1 *medium onion, chopped*
- 1 *clove garlic, chopped*
- 4 *tomatoes, peeled and chopped, page 34*
- 2 *chopped fresh chilies, pages 27–29, or chili powder to taste*
- 4 *tortillas*
- 4 *eggs*
- 4 *tablespoons grated Parmesan or Cheddar cheese*
- 1 *avocado (optional)*
- *Coarse salt and freshly ground pepper*

A superb dish for a late Sunday morning breakfast. The eggs can either be cooked in the chili mixture or fried separately.

• Heat 2 tablespoons of the lard in a skillet. Add the onion and garlic and cook until soft. Add the tomatoes and chilies and simmer until thick. Season.

In a separate pan heat the rest of the lard and fry the tortillas. Remove and drain. Fry the eggs (or make hollows in the sauce and break them in, cover and cook over low heat until done). Put an egg on each tortilla, spoon on some sauce, sprinkle with cheese, and garnish with slices of avocado. Serves 2–4.

HUEVOS CON CHORIZO

- 1 *tablespoon oil or butter*
- 2 *chorizos, skinned and chopped*
- 1 *medium onion, finely chopped*
- 3 *tomatoes, peeled and chopped,* *page* 34
- *Coarse salt and freshly ground pepper*
- 1 *fresh green chili, minced,* *pages* 27–29, *(optional)*
- 6 *eggs, lightly beaten*

Chorizos (hot sausages) are available at Mexican or Spanish groceries. Italian hot sausage can be substituted.

• Heat the oil in a heavy-bottomed skillet. Fry the sausage meat with the onion for about 5 minutes. Add the tomatoes, salt, pepper, chili, and cook for another 5 minutes. Stir the eggs into the mixture and cook over low heat, stirring with a wooden spoon for about 3 minutes. Serves 3.

SPANISH PEPPER OMELETTE

- 1 *red bell pepper*
- 1 *green bell pepper*
- 1 *fresh or canned green chili pepper,* *pages* 27–29
- 6 *eggs*
- *Coarse salt and freshly ground pepper*
- 3 *tablespoons olive oil*

A late breakfast or lunch dish, tomato and onion salad made with good Spanish olive oil would be good to follow.

• Chop the peppers and beat the eggs with the salt and pepper. Heat the oil in a frying pan and fry the peppers for about 5 minutes. Add the eggs and cook until barely firm. Serves 3.

CREOLE POACHED EGGS

- 1 *medium onion, finely chopped*
- 4 *tablespoons butter*
- 2 *green bell peppers, finely chopped*
- ¼ *pound mushrooms, sliced*
- *Coarse salt*
- *Freshly ground pepper*
- 1 *teaspoon Cayenne pepper*
- 1½ *cups chicken stock*
- 2 *cups Tomato Sauce, page 177 (or 2 small cans Italian tomatoes plus juice)*
- 1 *teaspoon vinegar*
- *Herb bouquet (parsley, thyme, bay leaf, tied in cheesecloth)*
- 3 *cloves*
- 8 *eggs*
- *Fresh chopped parsley to garnish*

Rice or hot French bread goes with this dish.

• Soften the onion in the butter in a large casserole. Add the peppers and cook for a few minutes, then add the mushrooms, salt, pepper, and Cayenne. Cook for a few more minutes, then add the stock, sauce, vinegar, herb bouquet, and cloves. Cover and simmer over very low heat for about 20 minutes. Carefully break in the eggs, one at a time. Cover and poach until the eggs are done. Remove herb bouquet, sprinkle with chopped parsley, and serve. Serves 4.

EGGS POACHED IN CURRY SAUCE

- 2 *tablespoons butter*
- 1 *medium onion, finely chopped*
- 2 *tablespoons Mild Curry Powder, page 40*
- 1 *tablespoon flour*
- 1 *cup tomato juice*
- 1 *cup chicken or vegetable stock*
- 1 *tablespoon chutney*
- 1 *tablespoon grated coconut*
- *Coarse salt and freshly ground pepper*
- *Poached eggs*

• Melt the butter in a heavy-bottomed skillet. Soften the onion, add the curry powder, cook for 2 minutes, add the flour, and cook 2 more minutes, taking care to prevent burning. Add the tomato juice and stock, chutney, coconut, salt, and pepper, and simmer for an hour. Set aside (this improves if kept overnight).

Poach the eggs by dropping them into boiling water. Fry rounds of bread.

Arrange the eggs on the fried bread and pour the sauce over them.

INDIAN SCRAMBLED EGGS

- 6 *eggs*
- *Coarse salt*
- *Freshly ground pepper*
- ¼ *cup milk*
- 3 *tablespoons ghee, page* 45, *or butter*
- 1 *medium onion, chopped*
- 1 *inch fresh ginger, finely chopped*
- *Fresh coriander (a handful), chopped*
- ½ *teaspoon turmeric*
- 2 *teaspoons fresh chilies, finely chopped*

Serve these with Chapattis, page 157.

• Beat the eggs in a bowl with salt, pepper, and milk. Heat the ghee or butter in a skillet and gently fry the onion with the ginger until soft. Add the coriander, turmeric, and chilies, and fry for another couple of minutes. Pour in the eggs, turn the heat way down, and cook very slowly, stirring. When the eggs are barely set, turn out and serve. Serves 3.

CURRY OMELETTE

- 8 *eggs*
- 4 *tablespoons ghee, page* 45, *or butter*
- 1 *medium onion, finely chopped*
- 1 *clove garlic, minced*
- ½ *teaspoon ground turmeric*
- ½ *teaspoon ground cumin*
- ½ *teaspoon ground coriander*
- ¼ *teaspoon ground ginger*
- 2 *green fresh chilies, minced, pages* 27–29
- *A little water*
- *Coarse salt and freshly ground pepper*
- 4 *tablespoons cooked meat, diced*

This is a combination of East-West cooking techniques. The sauce improves if made the night before. Make the omelettes in an omelette pan. I prefer to make individual omelettes but if you wish, you can make two large ones and cut them in half.

• Heat the butter or ghee in a saucepan and soften the onion with the garlic. Add the spices and chilies and cook for 2 minutes without burning. Add the water, salt, pepper, and meat. Cook for 5 minutes. Set aside.

Make the omelettes and just before they are ready (i.e., when they are still runny in the middle) spoon in some of the curry mixture. Fold over and serve at once. Serves 4.

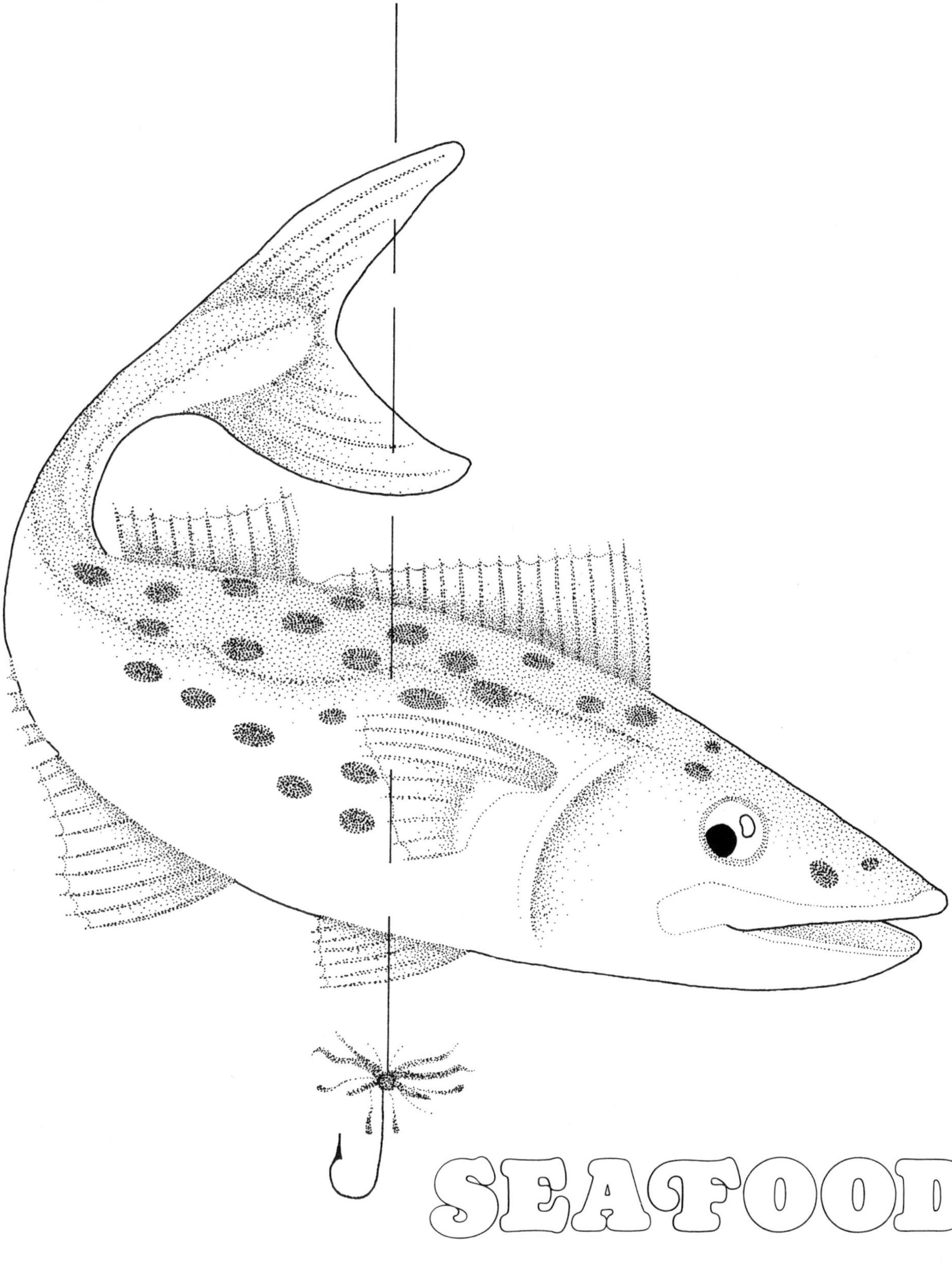

SEAFOOD

Some of the best dishes in the world are made from the fish along tropical coastlines. Hot peppers and spices, combined with lemon or lime juice, coconut milk, and fresh ginger, are used to marinate raw fish which is then either eaten raw or prepared in a variety of ways. The Chinese use sesame oil, hot peppers, garlic, and soy sauce; the Indonesians marinate fish in vinegar, oil, and coconut milk. The Moroccans are extraordinarily inventive with olives and preserved lemons; the Mexicans with capers, chilies, and pimiento-stuffed olives. The Indians prepare fish with a mixture of ground spices (masala), the Europeans with mustard and paprika. Many of the superb dishes that distinguish African, Creole, Asian, and Latin American cooking can be duplicated in the American kitchen. Spices should be freshly ground and no substitutes should be used.

Be sure to choose fish that have firm slithery flesh, bright eyes, rosy gills, and no smell. Avoid frozen fish if possible, particularly if there is a deposit of frozen juices at the bottom of the packet. This means it has been thawed and frozen again. Do not use frozen fish for marinated raw dishes.

MARINATED RED SNAPPER, GHANA-STYLE

- 2½–3 *pounds red snapper, filleted*
- *Juice of* 3 *lemons*
- ½ *cup olive oil*
- 4 *fresh chilies, prepared according to page* 29 *chopped*
- 2 *tablespoons fresh thyme*
- 2 *tablespoons fresh parsley, chopped*
- *Coarse salt and freshly ground pepper*
- ½ *cup fresh grated coconut*

This can be served as an appetizer or main course. The snapper must be extremely fresh.

• Slice the fillets into pieces about 2 × 3 inches. Marinate the fish in the lemon juice for three hours, or until it has turned opaque. Combine the remaining ingredients and toss the fish in this mixture. Serve chilled. Serves 4–6.

CANGREJOS ENCHILADOS (CRABS IN PEPPER SAUCE, DOMINICAN REPUBLIC)

1 pound fresh crabmeat
¼ cup olive oil
1 large onion, chopped
1 green bell pepper, chopped
3 cloves garlic, finely chopped
3 hot chilies, finely chopped, pages 27–29
6 medium tomatoes, peeled and chopped, page 34
3 tablespoons tomato purée
½ cup dry sherry
Coarse salt and freshly ground pepper
2 tablespoons lime juice
2 tablespoons chopped fresh parsley

Serve with plain boiled rice.

• Pick over the crabmeat to remove bits of shell or cartilage. In a heavy 12-inch skillet heat the oil. Cook the onion with the garlic, peppers, and chilies until tender. Add the tomatoes, tomato purée, sherry, salt, and pepper, and cook, stirring, for about 10 minutes. Add the lime juice, stir well, then add the crabmeat. Cook over very low heat, covered, for 2–3 minutes, just enough to heat the crabmeat. Do not overcook. Correct seasoning. Sprinkle with parsley and serve. Serves 4.

ESCOVITCH (JAMAICAN MARINATED FISH)

3 pounds red snapper, filleted (or any firm-fleshed white fish)
Coarse salt and freshly ground pepper
1 cup olive oil
4 medium onions, thinly sliced
2 bell peppers, cut into strips
2 cloves garlic, peeled
2 bay leaves
½ teaspoon crushed red pepper
¾ cup vinegar
¼ cup water

• Cut the fillets into 1½-inch pieces. Season and fry in 2–3 tablespoons of the olive oil. Transfer to a shallow serving dish.

Combine the rest of the ingredients (except the olive oil) in a heavy saucepan and simmer until the onion is cooked. Add the remaining oil, mix well, pour the mixture over the fish, and leave it to marinate in the refrigerator for at least a day before serving. Serves 6–8.

SZECHWAN SHRIMP

2 pounds shrimp
2 egg whites
2 tablespoons cornstarch
Peanut or vegetable oil for deep-frying
2 tablespoons sesame oil
2 cloves garlic, chopped
1 inch fresh ginger, chopped
3 scallions, chopped
2 teaspoons crushed red pepper
2 chili peppers, diced
2 tablespoons dry sherry
1 teaspoon soy sauce
¼ teaspoon sugar
1 tablespoon catchup
½ cup chicken broth
Coarse salt and freshly ground pepper

Rice, page 154, goes with this peppery shrimp dish. Beer is a good drink with it and a salad to follow (see Green Salad, page 163) makes it a complete meal.

• Shell and devein the shrimp. Beat the egg whites with a little salt until stiff and mix in the cornstarch. Coat the shrimp with this mixture and let stand for a few hours.

Deep-fry the shrimp in the peanut or vegetable oil, a few at a time in a basket, and drain on paper towels. Meanwhile, heat the sesame oil in a frying pan and stir-fry the garlic, ginger, scallions, red pepper, and chilies. Combine the sherry, soy sauce, sugar, catchup, broth, and seasonings in a bowl. Add the shrimp to the frying pan, pour in the sauce, and bring to a boil. Remove from heat and serve at once. Serves 4.

HUNGARIAN SHRIMPS PAPRIKASH

3 tablespoons shallots, chopped
4 tablespoons butter
2 pounds shrimp, peeled
Coarse salt
Freshly ground pepper
Cayenne
1½ tablespoons Hungarian paprika
½ cup heavy cream
½ cup sour cream
1 tablespoon Dijon-type mustard
Fresh chopped parsley to garnish

Plain rice and a green vegetable such as zucchini, peas, broccoli, string beans, or lima beans are good accompaniments here.

• Soften the shallots in the butter and add the shrimp. Cook for a few minutes, until barely turned pink, with the salt, pepper, Cayenne, and paprika added. Add the cream, sour cream, and the mustard, and heat through without boiling. Serve immediately, sprinkled with parsley. Serves 4.

SHRIMP WITH MUSTARD SAUCE

2 pounds shrimp
¾ cup dry white wine
1 lemon, sliced
4 sprigs of parsley
Bay leaf
Peppercorns
Coarse salt
2 tablespoons Dijon-type mustard
Juice of a lemon
¾ cup olive oil

This is a cold dish and may also be served as an hors d'oeuvre accompanied by toast. As a main course, Rice Salad, page 164, goes well and makes a good summer evening meal.

• Peel the shrimp. Heat the wine in a skillet with the lemon, parsley, bay leaf, and peppercorns. When it is boiling add the shrimps and cook only until they turn pink, turning them once. Remove the shrimp, reserving the wine.

In a small bowl beat the mustard with the lemon juice and gradually add the oil to make a thick mayonnaiselike sauce. Thin out with a little of the cooking wine as needed. Salt the shrimp and coat them with the mixture. Leave the shrimp to marinate overnight or for a few hours. Serves 4.

FISH STEAKS WITH CHILI SAUCE

Olive oil
2 medium onions, sliced
2 cloves garlic, sliced
4 red or green chili peppers, chopped, pages 27–29
6 tomatoes, chopped (or a 1-pound can of Italian tomatoes)
1 tablespoon fresh chopped basil (or dried)
½ teaspoon oregano
Coarse salt and freshly ground pepper
6 fish steaks (any kind)

Fried bananas or plantains, page 141, Mexican Beans, page 151, or rice all go with this Latin American dish. A green vegetable and hot French or Italian bread would also be good accompaniments.

• Coat the bottom of a large casserole with olive oil. Place the onions, garlic, and chilies in the oil and cook gently for about 5 minutes. Add the tomatoes, herbs, salt, and pepper. Season the steaks, place them on the mixture, and cover. Cook over medium heat on top of the stove. Baste frequently with the sauce and turn the steaks once so that they are fully cooked on both sides. Serves 4.

COD BROCHETTES WITH MUSTARD SAUCE

- 4 *thick cod steaks*
- *Coarse salt*
- *Plain white flour*
- *Cayenne pepper*
- *Oil for deep-frying*
- *Mustard Sauce, page 175*

• Make the mustard sauce and keep warm in the top of a double boiler. Cut fish into 1-inch squares and thread on small skewers. Salt the fish, flour them, and sprinkle with Cayenne. Deep-fry in very hot oil until golden. Serve at once with mustard sauce in a separate bowl.

AFRICAN STEWED FISH

- 4 *firm, white fish fillets, cut into pieces 2-inches square*
- *Flour for dredging*
- *Coarse salt and freshly ground pepper*
- ¼ *cup palm or peanut oil*
- 2 *medium onions, sliced*
- 4 *large tomatoes or a 1-pound can of tomatoes*
- 1 *teaspoon tomato paste*
- *Crushed red pepper to taste (about 1 tablespoon)*
- 1 *cup fish stock, page 50*
- *Fresh chopped basil or parsley*

It is much cheaper and you will get a better stew if you fillet the fish yourself. You can then simmer the bones and heads in water with an onion, peppercorns, bay leaf, and a chopped carrot for an hour, which will give you a good fish stock.

Serve this stew with rice or corn.

• Dredge the fish with seasoned flour. Heat the oil in a casserole and fry the fillets. Remove and drain. Add the onions, chopped tomatoes, and cook for 5 minutes. Add the tomato paste, crushed red pepper, and stock. Simmer gently for about 15 minutes. Add the fish and cook for a further 5 minutes. Correct seasoning and serve, sprinkled with chopped basil or parsley. Serves 4.

INDIAN FRIED FISH

- 1 *pound plaice, sole, or flounder (or any white, filleted fish)*
- 4 *tablespoons flour*
- 1 *egg*
- 2 *tablespoons water*
- 1 *teaspoon Garam Masala, page 40*
- ½ *teaspoon chili powder*
- *Oil for deep-frying*

The flour for the batter may be a combination of 2 tablespoons white flour and 2 tablespoons besan (split-pea flour), which can be bought in Indian shops. Ground yellow split peas make a good substitute.

• Cut the fillets into 2/3-inch strips. Season them with half the garam masala and chili powder. Combine the flour, egg, water, and remaining garam masala and dip the fish pieces into the mixture. Deep-fry in hot oil until golden. Serve with lemon pickle. Serves 2–4.

MOROCCAN RICE-STUFFED FISH

- 5 *pounds whole fish (red snapper, striped bass, halibut, grouper)*
- *Chermoula (Moroccan fish marinade), page 183*
- ½ *cup rice*
- 2 *pounds tomatoes*
- 6 *ounces pitted green olives,*
- 1 *Preserved Lemon, page 187*
- 2 *sticks butter*
- 2 *green chilies, prepared according to page 29*
- *Coarse salt and freshly ground pepper*

• Wash and clean the fish; the head and tail should be left on. Leave in the marinade for at least an hour, more if possible.

Parboil the rice for 5 minutes. Peel and seed the tomatoes, dice them, and reserve the juice. Parboil the olives, dice them, dice the lemon peel, and mix with the tomatoes and the chermoula. Add the parboiled rice to this mixture.

Put some butter in the inside of the fish, season with salt and pepper, add the chermoula-rice mixture, and secure the cavity with a skewer or sew with needle and thread. Cover the fish with remaining butter and chopped chilies. Pour on the tomato juice. Bake, covered, in a preheated 375-degree oven for about 1¼ hours. Serves 6.

MOROCCAN FISH WITH TOMATOES AND FENNEL STALKS

- 4½–5 *pounds fish (striped bass, red snapper, etc., left whole if small, or cut into steaks)*
- *Chermoula (Moroccan fish marinade), page 183*
- 3 *pounds tomatoes*
- 1 *teaspoon ginger*
- 1 *pinch pulverized saffron*
- 2 *cloves garlic, chopped*
- ½ *teaspoon ground chili*
- 2 *tablespoons olive oil*
- *Coarse salt and freshly ground pepper*
- 1 *Preserved Lemon, page 187*
- 6 *green olives, pitted*
- 8 *stalks fennel, leaves on*
- *Fresh chopped parsley to garnish*

Moroccans cook fish in a tajin, an earthenware pot with a conical lid, in which they lay pieces of cane to stop the fish from touching the bottom and burning. Carrots, celery, and fennel stalks can also be used for this, and the latter adds a delicious aroma to the fish. Use a heavy casserole and either bake this in the oven or cook it on the top of the stove.

• Wash the fish, pat it dry, and marinate for at least an hour in the chermoula. Peel and seed the tomatoes and put them, with their juice, in a saucepan. Add the ginger, saffron, garlic, chili, olive oil, salt, and pepper, and simmer gently, stirring frequently, until you have a thick purée. Add the lemon and olives and set aside.

Arrange the fennel stalks in a criss-cross pattern at the bottom of a tajin or heavy casserole. Place the fish on the fennel and pour on the remaining chermoula and the tomato purée. Cook on the top of the stove over medium-low heat for 30 minutes, or bake for 45 minutes at 350 degrees. Garnish with parsley and serve hot or cold. Serves 6.

POISSON EN BLAFF (GUADALOUPE)

½ cup fresh lime juice
3 cups water
1 hot chili, diced, pages 27–29
Coarse salt
3 cloves garlic
2 1-pound white fish (red snapper, etc., whole)
1 cup dry white wine
1 medium onion, chopped
2 cloves garlic, chopped
2 whole allspice berries
Fresh chopped parsley to garnish

• Combine the lime juice, 2 cups water, chili, salt, and garlic, and marinate the fish in this mixture for an hour. Discard marinade.

Bring the remaining cup of water to a boil, add the wine, onions, garlic, and allspice. Reduce heat and simmer, covered, for about 5 minutes.

Add the fish and simmer about 10 minutes, or until done. Pour the poaching liquid over the fish; squeeze on more lime juice if necessary. Correct seasoning, garnish with parsley, and serve. Serves 2–4.

DEEP-FRIED FISH SZECHWAN

2 pounds fish fillets
1 egg
6 tablespoons sherry
5 tablespoons flour
Coarse salt and freshly ground pepper
Peanut or vegetable oil for deep-frying
2 tablespoons sesame oil
1 cup bamboo shoots, chopped (or 1 small can)
1 chili, minced
1 scallion, chopped
½-inch piece fresh ginger, chopped
1 teaspoon vinegar
3 tablespoons soy sauce
1 cup fish or chicken stock
1 tablespoon cornstarch mixed to a paste with 1 tablespoon cold water

Use a firm-fleshed white fish (bass, halibut, etc). Rice, page 154, and a green vegetable are the best accompaniments.

• Cut the fish into 2-inch squares. Mix the egg with 4 tablespoons sherry, flour, salt, and pepper. Dip the fish fillets into this batter and deep-fry. Drain on paper towels.

Meanwhile heat the sesame oil in a frying pan and stir-fry the bamboo shoots, chili, scallion, and ginger. Add the vinegar and soy sauce. Cook for 2 minutes, then add the fish with the stock and remaining 2 tablespoons sherry. Bring to boil, add the cornstarch mixture, and cook for 2 minutes. Correct seasoning and serve. Serves 4.

MACKEREL WITH MUSTARD SAUCE

4 small or 2 large mackerel
Juice of 1 lemon
Coarse salt and freshly ground pepper
2 tablespoons olive oil
3 tablespoons shallots or scallions, chopped
3 tablespoons butter
1 teaspoon flour
½ cup dry white wine
4 tablespoons Dijon-type or dark mustard
Fresh chopped parsley

A green vegetable and rice go well with this dish.

• Clean the mackerel and squeeze the lemon juice on the cavities. Season, sprinkle with oil, and bake under a broiler.

Meanwhile cook the shallots in the butter without browning. Add the flour and cook for 2 minutes. Add the wine and mustard and stir thoroughly. Bring to a boil, stirring, and cook until thickened. Remove from heat, pour over the mackerel, and sprinkle with parsley. Serves 4.

INDONESIAN SPICED MACKEREL

4 small or 2 large mackerel
About 1 tablespoon red wine vinegar
2 tablespoons fresh chopped basil (or dried, if fresh is unavailable)
Peanut or vegetable oil
1 medium onion, chopped
¾ cup water
4 tablespoons fresh or canned green chili, chopped, pages 27–29
½ inch of fresh ginger, diced
2 cloves garlic, chopped
Coarse salt and freshly ground pepper to taste

Serve this with rice and grilled or stewed tomatoes.

• Clean the mackerel and put a little vinegar and basil in the cavities. Sprinkle with peanut oil and grill under a broiler.

Meanwhile combine the onion, water, chili, ginger, and garlic in a blender and purée. Heat about 3 tablespoons peanut oil in a skillet and fry the mixture over high heat, stirring constantly. Correct seasoning and keep warm.

When ready to serve, spoon the sauce over the mackerel. Serves 4.

BALINESE SPICED FISH

- 1 *3–4 pound whole fish (snapper, striped bass, any firm, white-fleshed fish)*
- 1 *teaspoon crushed chili peppers*
- *Juice of 1 lemon*
- ¼ *teaspoon ground allspice*
- 2 *cloves garlic, minced*
- 2 *tablespoons chopped fresh ginger*
- 2 *tablespoons soy sauce*
- 3 *scallions, including green part, chopped*
- ½ *cup peanut or vegetable oil*
- *Coarse salt and freshly ground pepper*

Serve with rice.

• Pat the fish dry with paper towels. Mix together all the remaining ingredients and coat the fish with the mixture, inside and out. Leave for at least an hour at room temperature.

Preheat oven to 375 degrees. Bake, covered, until done (about half an hour), turning once. Serves 4.

RED SNAPPER VERACRUZ

- 1 *3–4 pound red snapper, head on*
- *Juice of 1 lime or lemon*
- *Coarse salt and freshly ground black pepper*
- ½ *cup olive oil*
- 1 *medium onion, chopped*
- 2 *cloves garlic, chopped*
- ¾ *cup tomato purée*
- 5 *tomatoes, peeled and chopped, page 34*
- 4 *jalapeño chilies, fresh or canned, chopped, pages 27–29*
- ¼ *teaspoon cinnamon*
- ¼ *teaspoon ground cloves*
- 2 *teaspoons capers*
- 1 *cup fish stock or water*
- *Sliced pimiento-stuffed olives to garnish*

Mexican Beans, page 151, are good with this dish, as is rice.

• Rub the fish inside and out with the lemon juice and season. Heat the oil in a skillet and soften the onion with the garlic. Add the tomato purée, tomatoes, chilies, cinnamon, cloves, capers, and stock. Bring to a boil, turn down, and simmer gently for 10 minutes.

Put the fish in a poaching dish and cover with the sauce, putting some underneath it first so that it doesn't stick. Simmer until cooked. Remove to a heated dish, spoon the sauce over it, and decorate with the olives. Serves 4–6.

JAMAICAN FISH CAKES

½ pound salt cod
2 tablespoons Achiote Oil, page 43
2 medium onions, chopped
1 cup flour
1 teaspoon baking powder
Coarse salt
Freshly ground pepper
¾ cup milk
1 egg
1 tablespoon melted butter
2 small chilies, finely chopped

These fish cakes make a good cheap meal; they are filling and nutritious. Accompany them with a green vegetable such as spinach, broccoli, or zucchini, and rice, if you like.

Salt cod must be soaked overnight in several changes of water. I rinse it thoroughly each time. You can test its final saltiness by licking it. If it is not too salty after the final rinsing, I suggest cooking it in the milk instead of water and reserving the milk to use in the batter, cooling it first. If the fish is very salty, cook it in water (which you throw out), and don't salt the fish cakes.

• Simmer the fish for 20 minutes in water or milk until it flakes with a fork. Remove from heat and set aside. Heat the oil and fry the onions over low heat until soft. Set aside.

Sift the flour into a bowl with the baking powder and seasonings. Make a well in the middle and add the milk and beaten egg. Add the butter and mix well. Add the chilies, onions, and fish, and mix thoroughly. Fry a tablespoon of the batter at a time in oil in a skillet for about 2 minutes on each side. Remove to drain on paper towels and serve. Serves 4.

PAELLA

1½ pounds chicken, cut up
Olive oil
3 tomatoes, peeled and chopped, page 34
1 teaspoon Hungarian paprika or pimentón
½ teaspoon saffron powder
1 chorizo, sliced (Italian hot sausage may be substituted)
2 ounces string beans
2 cups long-grain rice
8 small shrimp, peeled
Coarse salt and freshly ground pepper
Fresh chopped parsley to garnish

If you do not own a special paella pan, use a skillet with a wide flat base, about 2 inches deep and 12 inches across.

• Fry the chicken pieces in the oil. Remove and set aside. Fry the tomatoes; stir in the paprika and chorizo. Add 5 cups water. Bring to a boil. Return the chicken, add beans, and simmer for about 10 minutes. Add the rice and saffron powder and cook for 15 minuters. Add the shrimp, more water if dry, and cook for a further 7 minutes. Correct seasoning. The grains of rice should be yellow and separate. Sprinkle with parsley and serve immediately. Serves 4.

KEDGEREE

½ pound long-grain rice
1 medium onion, chopped
1 stick butter
2 fresh chilies, cut in thin strips, pages 27–29
2 tablespoons fresh ginger, minced
¼ teaspoon turmeric
1 tablespoon Mild Curry Powder, page 40
1 pound cooked smoked haddock
4 hardboiled eggs, diced
2–3 tablespoons heavy cream
2 tablespoons chopped fresh parsley
Coarse salt and freshly ground pepper

This dish originated in India and became extremely popular in England where it is often made from smoked haddock. Other suitable fish include any white fish and salmon. This is my own version, a combination of Indian and British.

• Boil the rice until cooked and drain, page 154. Softten the onion in the butter without browning, add the chilies and ginger, and cook for 2 minutes. Add the turmeric, curry powder, and cook 2 more minutes. Add the fish and hardboiled eggs. Mix and heat through. Add the rice and stir with a fork. Stir in the cream just before serving and sprinkle with parsley. Serves 4–6.

POULTRY

There was a time when chicken was a luxury, but now it is one of the cheapest meats on the market. Unfortunately, the free-range bird which was so delicious when roasted simply with butter and tarragon has been replaced by the factory-raised hen, whose value is calculated down to the last minute of its life. Modern chickens never see the light of day; their feet never touch the ground. They sit immobilized in cages too small to turn in, where they are fed with artificial feeds and injected with hormones. Quite apart from the discouraging humanitarian aspect of this treatment, they offer little in terms of taste. Spices and aromatics have become essential if such chickens are to be palatable. Turmeric, saffron, paprika, and chilies give rich color and flavor to an otherwise dull bird.

Fresh chicken should have white, firm skin and no unpleasant smell. Check packaged chicken to make sure there is no deposit of frozen juices at the bottom. This means it has been frozen and thawed. Frozen poultry is often tough because it is put in the freezer too soon after it has been slaughtered. The best chicken comes from a good butcher or from a farmer who still raises free-range birds.

POULET DIJONNAIS

- 1 3–4 *pound chicken*
- *Fresh tarragon (if available–no substitute)*
- 2 *tablespoons Dijon-type mustard*
- 2 *tablespoons softened butter*
- ¼ *cup brandy*
- 1 *cup heavy cream*
- *Coarse salt*
- *Freshly ground white pepper*

A French dish, this goes well with rice and a green vegetable.

• Wipe the chicken with paper towels and put small pieces of tarragon under the skin. Combine the mustard and the butter and spread it over the chicken, putting a little of the mixture in the cavity. Season with salt and pepper and place in a roasting pan.

Roast in preheated 350-degree oven for about an hour, or until done. Remove to a plate and put the roasting pan on top of the stove. Bring the cooking juices to a boil, add the brandy, cook, stirring, for a minute or so, then add the cream. Heat through, correct seasoning, add more chopped tarragon, and pass the sauce separately in a sauceboat. Serves 4.

ROAST CHICKEN WITH PAPRIKA

- *1 3–4-pound roasting chicken*
- *2 tablespoons Hungarian paprika*
- *1 medium onion, sliced*
- *4 tablespoons chopped scallions or shallots*
- *1 stick butter*
- *1 cup dry white wine*
- *Coarse salt and freshly ground pepper*
- *2 tablespoons flour*
- *1 cup hot chicken stock*
- *1 cup heavy cream*
- *Fresh parsley to garnish*

The paprika will make the chicken roast deep golden brown. Serve this with rice and a green vegetable.

• Sprinkle the chicken with half the paprika, rub into the flesh, and leave at room temperature for a couple of hours. Arrange in a deep casserole (the kind that also goes on top of the stove) with the sliced onion, and put pieces of butter in the cavity and on the breast. Roast, basting frequently, until done (about an hour). The juices will run clear and yellow when the chicken is pricked by a fork. Remove and keep warm.

Add the scallions or shallots and soften in the casserole with the remaining butter. Add the remaining paprika and the flour. Cook together for a couple of minutes without burning. Add the stock, wine, and bring to a boil. Simmer for about 10 minutes, until thick. Add the cream and heat through. Correct seasoning. Garnish sauce with parsley and serve in a sauce-boat. Serves 4.

CHICKEN PAPRIKASH

- *1 3–3½-pound chicken, cut up*
- *2 tablespoons lard or bacon fat*
- *2 cloves garlic, chopped*
- *2 medium onions, chopped*
- *1 green bell pepper, chopped*
- *1½ tablespoons Hungarian paprika*
- *1 cup chicken stock*
- *2 tablespoons flour*
- *1 cup sour cream*

Serve this Hungarian dish with noodles, rice, or Hungarian Dumplings, page 158. A green salad would be good to follow.

• Dry the chicken with paper towels. Brown chicken pieces in the fat. Remove and drain on paper towels. In the same pan, fry the garlic and the onion without browning. Add the pepper and fry for a minute. Off heat, stir in the paprika. Add the chicken stock and return the chicken pieces to the pan. Cover and cook over medium heat for about 25–30 minutes, or until chicken is done. Remove the chicken and skim off as much fat as you can.

Mix the flour with ¼ cup sour cream until smooth and add. Bring to a boil and cook until thick. Return the chicken to the sauce, add the remaining sour cream, and heat through but do not allow to boil. Serves 4.

DEVILLED CHICKEN LEGS

- 4 *whole chicken legs*
- *Melted butter*
- ½ *cup breadcrumbs*
- 1 *teaspoon dry mustard*
- 1 *teaspoon Mild Curry Powder, page 40*
- 1 *teaspoon Cayenne*
- *Coarse salt*
- *Freshly ground pepper*

Serve these with Piquant Mayonnaise, page 182. A green vegetable such as broccoli, peas, or braised celery would go well with them.

• Score the flesh on the skinned chicken legs. Dip into melted butter, then into the breadcrumbs seasoned with remaining ingredients. Arrange on broiling pan and cook under a hot broiler, basting with more melted butter as you go. Serves 4.

MOROCCAN STEAMED CHICKEN

- 2 *3-pound chickens*
- 10 *small white onions*
- ½ *cup chopped parsley*
- 1 *stick butter, softened*
- ¼ *teaspoon pulverized saffron*
- *Coarse salt*
- *Cumin*
- ¼ *teaspoon ground chilies (optional)*

• Dry the chickens thoroughly with paper towels. Parboil the onions in their skins and peel them. Fill the cavities of the chicken with the onions, parsley, and half the butter. Pound saffron with remaining butter and salt and rub into the skins. Bring water in steamer or couscoussière to boil. Arrange chickens in top and cover with cheesecloth. Steam about 1 hour, without lifting the lid.

Serve with bowls of cumin (mixed with chilies if you like) and coarse salt. Serves 6.

MOROCCAN CHICKEN WITH LEMON AND OLIVES

- 2 *chickens, cut up, with livers*
- *Coarse salt and freshly ground pepper*
- 1 *teaspoon ginger*
- 2 *tablespoons olive oil*
- 4 *tablespoons butter*
- 1 *medium onion, cut in half*
- 2 *cloves garlic, peeled*
- ¼ *teaspoon pulverized saffron*
- 8 *sprigs coriander, tied together*
- 2½ *cups water*
- 1 *Preserved Lemon, page 187*
- 10 *reddish brown olives (use Greek Kalamatas or Italian Gaetas)*

• Put the chickens and livers in a heavy casserole. Salt and pepper to taste, add ginger, oil, butter, onion, garlic, saffron, coriander, and water. Bring to a boil and simmer gently, partially covered, for about 30 minutes, basting often.

Remove chicken and keep warm. Put the livers, garlic, and onion in blender and reduce to a purée. Return to the casserole with the quartered lemon peel and olives. Bring to a boil and when thick pour over the chicken. Serves 6.

DJEJ M'HAMMER (MOROCCAN FRIED CHICKEN)

- *2 chickens, whole, with livers*
- *Coarse salt and freshly ground pepper*
- *2 cloves garlic, peeled*
- *1 medium onion, quartered*
- *¼ teaspoon pulverized saffron*
- *1 tablespoon paprika*
- *1 teaspoon cumin*
- *¼ teaspoon turmeric*
- *1 stick butter*
- *Bunch coriander*
- *2 cups water*
- *1 tablespoon olive oil*

• Put the chickens in a heavy pan with the livers. Add salt, pepper, garlic, onion, spices, half of the butter, and coriander. Add water and simmer 1 hour, basting frequently. Remove chicken.

Mash the onion in blender with livers and garlic and return to sauce. Set over high heat to reduce.

Meanwhile heat remaining butter and oil in frying pan. Brown the chickens.

Arrange in serving dish and pour the sauce on top. Serve immediately. Serves 6.

DJEJ MECHOUI (CHARCOAL BROILED CHICKEN, MOROCCAN-STYLE)

- *4 scallions, white part only*
- *2 cloves garlic, peeled*
- *Coarse salt and freshly ground pepper*
- *2 tablespoons chopped coriander*
- *1½ teaspoons paprika*
- *1 teaspoon cumin*
- *¼ teaspoon ground chilies, pages 27–29*
- *1 stick butter, softened*
- *2 broiling chickens, cut in quarters*

• With a mortar and pestle mash the scallions, garlic, salt, pepper, coriander, paprika, cumin, and chilies with the butter until you have a smooth paste. Cover the chickens with the mixture and set aside for a couple of hours.

Heat charcoal or broiler. Arrange the chickens skin side toward heat and baste until done, turning once. Serves 4.

very good

DJEJ KDRAS
(MOROCCAN CHICKEN WITH CHICK PEAS)

- ½ *cup dried chick peas, cooked, or 10-ounce can*
- 2 *chickens*
- ¼ *teaspoon pulverized saffron*
- *Coarse salt and freshly ground pepper*
- 3 *medium onions, sliced*
- 1 *cinnamon stick*
- 2½ *cups water*
- *Parsley sprigs, tied together*
- 1 *stick butter*
- *Juice of a lemon*

This is a Moroccan stew in which the chicken is cooked with smen, a strong Moroccan butter, together with onions, paprika, and saffron, with lemon juice squeezed on at the end. Ordinary butter will do as a substitute.

• Soak the dried chick peas overnight, drain, and simmer them in fresh water for an hour. Drain and peel. Put the chicken and chick peas into a heavy casserole. (If using canned chick peas do not add until chicken is cooked.) Add half the saffron, salt and pepper, 1 onion, cinnamon stick, water, parsley, and butter. Simmer for 30 minutes.

Add remaining onion and saffron. Cook 30 minutes more. (Add canned chick peas at this point.) Remove chicken. Reduce sauce, add lemon juice, correct seasoning, pour over the chicken, and serve. Serves 4–6.

POLLO VERDE
(MEXICAN CHICKEN WITH GREEN TOMATOES AND PUMPKIN SEEDS)

- 1 *3½–4-pound chicken, cut up*
- 2 *cups chicken stock*
- 1 *10-ounce can Mexican green tomatoes*
- 1 *medium onion, chopped*
- 2 *cloves garlic, peeled*
- 5 *canned serrano chilies, pages 27–29*
- ½ *cup chopped fresh coriander, plus additional sprigs to garnish*
- 1 *cup pepitas, ground*
- *Coarse salt and freshly ground pepper*
- 2 *tablespoons bacon fat, lard, or olive oil*

Serve with rice. Grind the pepitas (pumpkin seeds) in a spice grinder or electric blender—without liquid.

• Simmer the chicken in the stock for 30 minutes. Drain, set aside, and reserve the stock. In a blender grind the green tomatoes (with their liquid), onion, garlic, chilies, and coriander.

Heat the fat in a large heavy skillet and pour the mixture in. Add the pepitas and enough chicken stock to the sauce to make it as thick as heavy cream. Simmer for 15 minutes, adding more stock if necessary. Season with salt and pepper.

Put the chicken pieces in this sauce and simmer gently for 15 minutes. Garnish with coriander sprigs and serve. Serves 4–6.

POLLO TABASQUENO (TABASCO-STYLE CHICKEN)

1 4½–5-pound chicken, cut up
Juice of 1 lime, or ½ lemon, or ½ orange
6 tablespoons olive oil
4 medium onions, chopped
5 cloves garlic, minced
5 tomatoes, peeled and chopped
2 tablespoons green olives, chopped
1 anchovy, diced
1 tablespoon capers
2 tablespoons seedless raisins
4 prunes, pitted and chopped
¼ pound ham, chopped
½ teaspoon chili powder
2 tablespoons red wine vinegar
4 cloves
1 cinnamon stick
1½ cups chicken stock
Coarse salt and freshly ground pepper
½ cup slivered almonds
3 canned pimientos, cut into strips

• Rub the chicken with the lime, lemon, or orange juice. Brown in the oil; add the remaining ingredients, except the almonds and pimientos, and simmer for an hour, or until the chicken is tender. Garnish with slivered almonds and pimiento strips. Serves 6.

POLLO EN MOLE VERDE (MEXICAN CHICKEN IN GREEN MOLE SAUCE)

2 2½-pound chickens
3 cups water
1 medium onion
1 carrot

Sauce

4 poblano chilies, fresh or canned, (if fresh, see page 29 for instructions)
½ cup pepitas (pumpkin seeds)
½ cup walnuts
½ cup almonds
2 10-ounce cans Mexican green tomatoes
½ cup fresh coriander, chopped
1 clove garlic, peeled
Coarse salt and freshly ground pepper
2 tablespoons lard

• Simmer the chicken in the water with the onion and carrot for about 30 minutes. Drain and reserve the stock.

Meanwhile prepare the chilies and combine in a blender with the pepitas, walnuts, almonds, tomatoes (including the juice), coriander, and garlic. Blend to a smooth purée and season with salt and pepper.

Heat the lard in a large pan and add the sauce. Bring to a boil and add the cooking liquid from the chickens until the sauce is the consistency of heavy cream. Cut the chickens into pieces and add to the sauce. Heat through and serve. Serves 6.

KOREAN STEWED CHICKEN

- 2 2½-*pound chickens*
- ¾ *cup sesame oil*
- ½ *cup soy sauce (preferably Tamari)*
- 4 *scallions, chopped*
- 3 *cloves garlic, minced*
- 2–3 *tablespoons Korean red pepper or chili powder*
- *Coarse salt to taste*

• Cut the chickens into pieces. Combine the remaining ingredients and pour the sauce over the chicken, coating the pieces well. Leave to marinate for at least 2 hours, overnight if possible.

Put the chicken and the sauce in a heavy casserole and simmer gently on top of the stove for 1 hour, turning occasionally. Do not add any liquid—there will be sufficient. Serves 6.

CHICKEN IN CHILI-WALNUT SAUCE

- 1 3–4-*pound chicken, cut up*
- *Water to cover*
- 5 *fresh green chilies, pages 27–29*
- 2 *tablespoons peanut, sesame, or vegetable oil*
- 4 *ounces shelled walnuts*
- 4 *ounces shelled peanuts*
- 2 *slices bread, crusts removed*
- 2 *medium onions, peeled and coarsely sliced*
- 2 *cloves garlic, peeled*
- 2 *thick slices fresh ginger*
- ½ *teaspoon mace*
- ½ *teaspoon ground cinnamon*
- 2 *cloves*
- *Coarse salt and freshly ground pepper to taste*
- *Sesame seeds*
- *Coriander or parsley to garnish*

• Simmer the chicken in water until almost done. Drain and cool, reserving liquid. Toast the chilies, wrap in paper towels, and set aside. In the oil fry the walnuts, peanuts, and bread until lightly browned. Combine in a blender with the chilies, onions, garlic, ginger, spices, salt, and pepper. Add a cup of the chicken broth and purée.

Thin the mixture with 2 cups of broth and return to pan. Bring to a boil. Add chicken and simmer for about 20 minutes, until thick. Sprinkle with sesame seeds and fresh chopped coriander or parsley and serve. Serves 4.

CHICKEN SATÉ

4 chicken breasts
3 tablespoons ketjap manis, page 24, or soy sauce
2 tablespoons lime juice
1 clove garlic, minced
2 tablespoons vegetable or peanut oil

Serve satés made from different meats as a main course and accompany them with small bowls of rice, vegetables, chutneys, pages 188–189, sambals, page 190, and slices of orange.

Peanut Saté Sauce, page 181, Chili, Onion, and Tomato Sambal, page 190, or Indonesian Cucumber Relish, page 191, are all good accompaniments to this saté.

• Skin and bone the chicken breasts and cut them into ¾-inch squares. Marinate them in the ketjap, lime juice, and garlic for a few hours.

Thread the chicken pieces on skewers, brush with oil, and grill over hot coals or under a broiler.

CHICKEN WITH MACADAMIA NUTS

6 Macadamia nuts
1 teaspoon coriander seeds
¼ teaspoon turmeric
2 cloves garlic, minced
1½ medium onions, chopped
6 fresh chilies, chopped, pages 27–29
2 tablespoons peanut oil
1 3-pound chicken, cut up
3 cups Coconut Milk, page 44
2 tablespoons chopped lemon rind
2 tablespoons soy sauce or ketjap manis, page 24
1 tablespoon brown sugar
Coarse salt and freshly ground pepper

• Grind the nuts, coriander, and turmeric in a spice grinder or with a mortar and pestle. Mash the garlic, onions, and chilies to a fine paste either in a blender or with mortar and pestle. Set aside.

Heat the oil in a deep, heavy-bottomed skillet and fry the chicken until lightly browned. Set aside. Fry the spices for 2–3 minutes, stirring to prevent burning. Add the onion mixture and cook 5 minutes, without browning. Add the coconut milk, sugar, salt, and pepper, bring to a boil, return the chicken pieces to the pan (with any juices that might have run out), and simmer, covered, for 20–30 minutes, or until chicken is tender. Serves 4.

TURKEY MOLE POBLANO (TURKEY PUEBLA-STYLE)

- 1 *8–9-pound turkey, jointed and cut into pieces*
- *Water to cover*
- 4 *tablespoons lard*
- 6 *ancho chilies, page 28*
- 4 *pasilla chilies, page 28*
- 6 *mulato chilies, page 28*
- 2 *slices white homemade-type bread*
- ¼ *pound almonds*
- ¼ *pound shelled peanuts*
- 2 *medium onions, chopped*
- 3 *tomatoes, peeled and chopped, page 34*
- 3 *cloves garlic, chopped*
- ½ *teaspoon ground cinnamon*
- ½ *teaspoon ground cloves*
- ½ *teaspoon anise*
- ½ *teaspoon ground coriander*
- 1 *teaspoon sugar*
- 1 *1-ounce square unsweetened chocolate*
- *Coarse salt and freshly ground black pepper*
- 3 *tablespoons sesame seeds*

In Mexico this dish is made on special occasions. Chicken can also be used. Serve it with Guacamole, page 66, tortillas, rice, and Mexican Black Beans, page 150.

For a shortcut mole sauce, see page 179.

• Simmer the turkey pieces in water to cover for about an hour. Drain and pat dry. Heat the lard in a heavy skillet and brown the turkey. Remove and drain.

Meanwhile prepare the chilies according to page 29. Pour 2 cups of the turkey broth over them and soak them for 30 minutes.

In an electric blender grind the chilies, bread, almonds, peanuts, onions, tomatoes, and garlic to a coarse purée. Add the cinnamon, cloves, anise, coriander, and sugar. In the lard remaining in the skillet fry the mixture for 5 minutes, stirring constantly. Add 2 cups of turkey broth, chocolate, salt, and pepper. Bring to a boil.

Arrange the turkey pieces in an ovenproof dish. Pour the sauce over, cover, and bake at 350 degrees for about 45 minutes. Sprinkle with sesame seeds and serve. Serves 8–10.

AJÍ DE GALLINA (PERUVIAN CHICKEN WITH CHILIES)

- *1 4-pound chicken, cut up*
- *Water to cover*
- *1 stalk celery (with leaves), chopped*
- *3 medium onions, chopped*
- *2 carrots, chopped*
- *8 slices fresh homemade-type white bread*
- *2 cups milk*
- *⅔ cup oil*
- *2 cloves garlic, chopped*
- *2 tablespoons dried red chilies*
- *1 tablespoon achiote seeds, see note on page 72*
- *1 cup walnuts*
- *Coarse salt and freshly ground black pepper*
- *⅓ cup freshly grated Parmesan cheese*
- *3 hardboiled eggs, quartered*
- *12 black olives*
- *2 fresh hot chilies or pimientos, cut in thin strips, see pages 27–29*

Its bright colors and attractive patterns make this dish especially good for entertaining. It can be made in advance and heated through.

A salad is all you need to go with it. See page 163 for Green Salad.

• Simmer the chicken in the water with the celery, 1 onion, and carrots for about half an hour. Drain and reserve stock for another use. Skin, bone, and slice the chicken into thin strips.

Soak the bread in 1 cup of milk for 5 minutes. With your hands mash the bread and milk together to make a thick paste.

Heat the oil in a heavy skillet. Cook the remaining onions with the garlic for 5 minutes without browning. Meanwhile combine the dried chilies, achiote, and walnuts in a blender and grind fine. Add the bread paste and remaining cup of milk. Pour into the skillet and simmer, stirring, until the sauce thickens. Add the chicken and cheese and heat through.

Serve the mixture in a large, deep dish with the eggs, olives, and fresh chilies arranged in a spokelike pattern on top. Serves 4–6.

MEAT

Most of the dishes in this chapter are excellent for entertaining, since they improve if they are left overnight to develop their flavors. People with little time to cook after work can make them over a weekend or the night before.

It is more economical to buy large cuts of meat and cut them up yourself into the portions you need for stewing, etc. Buying meat from a butcher instead of at a supermarket may be more expensive, but in the long run you may well save money, since he can suggest the correct cuts for the dishes you are making. Marinated meat can be kept for several days in the refrigerator and its flavor vastly improved. Freezing robs meat of taste and texture.

BEEF

The best beef is marbled with fat, a deep red, and surrounded by a creamy layer of fat. If the meat is dark, dry, and the fat is yellow, it is old and stale. If packaged meat looks shiny and damp, it may have been frozen and thawed.

LAMB

Lamb absorbs flavor very well and is delicious with aromatic spices such as cumin, coriander, sesame seeds, paprika, and chili peppers. It becomes very tender when marinated. Good lamb has pale red flesh, white fat, and slightly translucent bones.

PORK

Pork responds quite well to marinades and is very good with chilies and hot spicy sauces. It has plenty of fat. It should be firm, pale pink, with no smell.

VEAL

Veal should be a very pale pink with firm, satiny fat. Do not buy dark veal—it has not been fed solely on milk. Veal has such a delicate flavor that it is a waste to cook such expensive meat in fiery sauces. The veal recipes in this chapter are therefore spicy but not overpowering.

SPICED BEEF SATÉ

2 pounds beef steak (any cut)
1 tablespoon coriander seeds
2 fresh chilies, coarsely chopped, pages 27–29
1 teaspoon turmeric
1 tablespoon fresh ginger, coarsely chopped
2 cloves garlic, peeled
1 medium onion, coarsely chopped
4 Macadamia nuts
Melted ghee, page 45 or peanut oil
1 cup Coconut Milk, page 44
1 tablespoon brown sugar
2 tablespoons grated lemon peel
Coarse salt and freshly ground pepper

• Cut the beef into 1-inch cubes. In an electric blender combine the coriander, chilies, turmeric, ginger, garlic, onion, and Macadamia nuts. Add ghee or oil to keep the blades turning.

Heat a tablespoon of ghee or oil in a heavy skillet. Add the mixture and fry until thick. Pour in coconut milk, sugar, lemon peel; season with salt and pepper, and bring to a boil. Remove from heat.

Thread the beef cubes on small skewers (preferably wooden oriental skewers) and grill under broiler or over hot coals, brushing generously with the sauce. Cook for 2–3 minutes, turning once. Serve the remainder of the sauce separately. Serve with rice. Serves 4–6.

KEFTA (MOROCCAN MEATBALLS)

1½ pounds ground beef or lamb (or mixture)
1 small onion, grated
1 teaspoon ground cuminseed
2 teaspoons paprika
¼ cup chopped parsley and fresh coriander
½ teaspoon Ras el Hanout, page 43 (optional)
2 sprigs fresh mint, chopped
¼ teaspoon ground cinammon
Coarse salt and freshly ground pepper

These meatballs are made with ground spiced lamb or beef and are put on skewers and grilled over charcoal. You can vary the flavors. Ras el Hanout (Moroccan spiced pepper) is often used. When you have spiced the meat, leave it for an hour or so so that the flavor has time to develop.

The meat must contain at least 10 percent fat. You can grind your own at home in a meat grinder.

• Combine all the ingredients in a mixing bowl. With wet hands, form mixture into 24 oblong-shaped patties and wrap them around skewers. Grill rapidly over high heat. Serves 6.

STIR-FRIED BEEF SZECHWAN-STYLE

- 1 *pound butt steak*
- 3 *tablespoons dry sherry*
- 3 *tablespoons soy sauce*
- 3 *tablespoons sesame oil*
- 2 *cloves garlic, minced*
- 2 *tablespoons minced fresh gingerroot*
- 3 *scallions, chopped (including green part)*
- ½ *teaspoon ground Szechwan pepper*
- *Coarse salt*

The cheaper cuts of steak are excellent here since this method of cooking prevents the meat from becoming tough.

• Slice the steak against the grain into thin strips. Combine the sherry, soy sauce, 2 tablespoons sesame oil, garlic, and ginger, and marinate the meat in this mixture for at least an hour (overnight if possible). Heat the remaining tablespoon of oil in a wok or skillet. Stir-fry the beef, including the marinade juice, for 2–3 minutes with the scallions. Do not overcook the meat or it will toughen. Season with salt and Szechwan pepper. Serve with boiled rice. Serves 2–4.

PICADILLO (CUBAN-STYLE HASH)

- 2 *pounds chopped lean beef*
- 4 *tablespoons Achiote Oil, page* 43
- *Coarse salt and freshly ground pepper*
- 2 *medium onions, finely chopped*
- 4 *green bell peppers, chopped*
- 2 *fresh chilies, chopped, pages* 27–29
- 2 *cloves garlic, finely chopped*
- 6 *tomatoes, peeled and chopped, page* 34
- 2 *cloves*
- 2 *apples, peeled and chopped*
- ½ *cup raisins*
- 6 *pimiento-stuffed olives, halved*
- ¼ *teaspoon ground cinnamon*
- 2 *tablespoons red wine vinegar*
- ¼ *cup slivered almonds*

Serve with fried eggs, Fried Plantains, page 141, boiled rice, Mexican Beans, page 151, as you choose.

• Brown the meat in the oil. Add the onions, peppers, chilies, garlic, salt, and pepper, and cook for about 3 minutes, taking care to prevent burning. Add remaining ingredients except almonds and simmer about 25 minutes. Meanwhile fry the almonds in a little oil. Sprinkle over the meat. Serve immediately. Serves 4–6.

MOROCCAN BEEF TAJINE WITH CAULIFLOWER

- 3 *pounds stewing beef (or lamb) cut into 1-inch cubes*
- ¼ *teaspoon turmeric*
- *Coarse salt and freshly ground pepper*
- ¼ *cup peanut oil*
- 1 *medium onion, chopped*
- 1 *teaspoon ground ginger*
- *Pinch pulverized saffron*
- 1 *tablespoon paprika*
- 1 *teaspoon cumin*
- ¼ *teaspoon Cayenne pepper*
- 2½ *pounds cauliflower*
- *Juice of 1 lemon*

• Put the beef in a heavy casserole with the turmeric, salt, pepper, and oil. Brown, turn heat down, cover tightly, and simmer for 15 minutes. Add onion and remaining spices, moisten with a little water, and simmer 1½ hours, adding more water if necessary.

Steam the cauliflower, broken into flowerets, until tender, set aside.

When meat is done, transfer to an ovenproof dish with its sauce. Arrange the cauliflower over the top and bake for 15 minutes in a hot oven. Remove cover and allow cauliflower to brown. Squeeze on the lemon juice and serve. Serves 6–8.

ROPA VIEJA (CUBAN FLANK STEAK)

- 2 *pounds flank steak*
- 2 *medium onions, chopped*
- 1 *carrot, sliced*
- 1 *turnip, peeled and cubed*
- 1 *bay leaf*
- *Water to cover*
- 3 *tablespoons Achiote Oil, page 43*
- 2 *cloves garlic, minced*
- 1 *hot fresh chili pepper, chopped, pages 27–29*
- 1 *green bell pepper, chopped*
- 6 *tomatoes, peeled and chopped, page 34*
- ⅛ *teaspoon ground cinnamon*
- ⅛ *teaspoon ground cloves*
- *Coarse salt and freshly ground pepper*
- 1 *tablespoon capers*
- 2 *canned pimientos, drained and finely chopped*

Serve with Fried Plantains, page 141, or Moors and Christians (Cuban Black Beans and Rice), page 156.

• Put the steak in a heavy casserole with 1 onion, the carrot, turnip, bay leaf, and pour in enough water to cover. Simmer for 1½ hours. When cool, shred it into pieces ¼ inch wide and 2 inches long. Set meat and liquid aside.

Pour the oil into the casserole and fry the remaining onion, the garlic, chili pepper, and bell pepper. Watch carefully to prevent burning. Add the tomatoes and remaining spices. Season with salt and pepper. Cook until sauce is thick. Return meat to casserole with 2 cups of its cooking liquid. Simmer for 5 minutes. Add the capers. Garnish with pimiento and serve. Serves 4–6.

BEEF GOULASH

- 3 *tablespoons lard or bacon fat*
- 3 *pounds stewing beef, cut in 1½-inch cubes*
- 4 *medium onions, finely chopped*
- 2 *cloves garlic, finely chopped*
- 2 *tablespoons paprika*
- 1 *cup dry red wine*
- 1 *cup beef stock*
- *Coarse salt*
- *Freshly ground pepper*
- 1 *teaspoon marjoram*
- *Herb bouquet (parsley, thyme, celery leaves, bay leaf, tied in cheesecloth)*
- 2 *tablespoons flour*

Serve this Hungarian stew with noodles. Use Hungarian paprika.

• Heat the fat in a heavy casserole that will go both on top of and inside the stove. Fry the onions until golden with the garlic. Off heat, stir in the paprika and add the beef. Pour in the wine, stock, salt, pepper, and herbs. Cook in a preheated 350-degree oven for 1 hour. Skim off 2 tablespoons fat and mix with the flour. Add the mixture to the stew and return to the oven for a further 30–40 minutes, or until beef is very tender. Remove herb bouquet before serving. Serves 4–6.

STEAK AU POIVRE

4 boneless steaks (sirloin or filet mignon)
⅓ cup peppercorns
3 tablespoons butter
1 tablespoon oil
½ cup white wine
¼ cup brandy
¼ cup heavy cream
Coarse salt

This famous French dish consists of steaks cooked briskly with the coarse crushed peppercorns pressed into either side. To crush the peppercorns either use a pestle and mortar (a peppermill will grind them too fine) or put them in a cloth and smash them with the back of a heavy frying pan or with a hammer.

Serve the steaks with baked potatoes.

• Trim the steaks and crush the peppercorns. With the heel of your hand press the peppercorns firmly into the meat on both sides of the steaks. Heat the butter and oil in a heavy frying pan and cook the steaks over high heat. Remove to a warm plate. Add the wine, bring to boil, add the brandy, cook for a minute (enough to boil off the alcohol), scraping up the cooking juices. Add the cream, heat through, season with salt, and pour over the steaks. Serves 4.

MEATBALLS PAPRIKASH

4 tablespoons butter
1 medium onion, chopped
1 clove garlic, chopped
1 pound ground beef
Coarse salt
Freshly ground pepper
1 egg
⅓ cup soft breadcrumbs
2 tablespoons chopped parsley
1 tablespoon paprika
1 tablespoon flour
1 cup beef stock
1 tablespoon tomato paste
¾ cup sour cream

A popular Czechoslovakian and Hungarian dish, serve it with noodles.

• Melt a tablespoon of butter and fry the onion with the garlic without browning. Combine in a bowl with the beef, salt, pepper, egg, breadcrumbs, and parsley. Shape into 1-inch balls.

Heat remaining butter in pan and fry the balls until brown all over. Remove to a warm plate. Add the paprika and flour and scrape up cooking juices. Add the stock and tomato paste and bring to a boil. Season with salt and pepper, and when thickened, turn down heat. Add the meatballs and sour cream, heat through, and serve. Serves 4.

Note: Meat freshly ground at home with a meat grinder makes meatballs vastly superior to those made with ready-ground hamburger.

SZÉKELY GULYÁS (PORK AND SAUERKRAUT GOULASH)

- 2 *tablespoons lard or bacon fat*
- 2 *medium onions, chopped*
- 1 *clove garlic, chopped*
- 1½ *tablespoons Hungarian paprika*
- *Coarse salt*
- *Freshly ground pepper*
- 2 *cups chicken or meat stock*
- 2 *pounds boneless pork, cut in 1-inch cubes*
- 1 *pound sauerkraut, washed and drained*
- 1 *tablespoon caraway seeds*
- 2 *tablespoons tomato purée*
- 1 *cup dry white wine*
- ½ *cup sour cream*
- ½ *cup heavy cream*
- 1 *tablespoon flour*

A famous goulash from Transylvania, the trick is not to dry out the sauerkraut. I suggest using a trivet under the casserole. Mashed potatoes and a bowl of sour cream are traditional accompaniments.

• Heat the fat in a casserole and sauté the onions with the garlic until golden. Off heat, stir in the paprika. Season with salt and pepper and add about ½ cup stock, stir, then add the pork. Arrange the sauerkraut in a layer over the pork, sprinkle with caraway seeds. Mix the tomato purée with the wine and remaining stock. Add, bring to a boil, turn down, and simmer 1 hour over very low heat, covered. Meanwhile mix the sour cream and heavy cream with the flour until smooth. Add to the casserole, bring to a boil, and cook for a few minutes. Remove and serve. Serves 4–6.

BEEF STROGANOFF

- 2 *pounds stewing beef, cut in 1½-inch cubes*
- 2 *tablespoons flour*
- 2 *tablespoons Hungarian paprika*
- 1 *stick butter*
- 2 *medium onions, chopped*
- 2 *cups beef stock*
- *Coarse salt and freshly ground pepper*
- 1 *cup sour cream*
- *Parsley to garnish*

Russian stroganoff does not contain either tomatoes or mushrooms. Serve this stew with noodles or boiled potatoes sprinkled with fresh chopped dill.

• Dredge the meat with the flour mixed with paprika. Heat the butter in a heavy-bottomed casserole and brown the meat. Remove. Soften the onions in the butter. Return the meat to the casserole with the stock and simmer gently for 2 hours, or until meat is tender. Stir in the sour cream and heat through, but do not allow to boil. Sprinkle with chopped parsley and serve. Serves 4–6.

Note: If you burn the butter when you are browning the meat, clean the casserole and use fresh butter for the onions.

TRINIDAD PEPPER POT

- 3–4 *pounds stewing chicken, cut up*
- 1 *pig's foot, split*
- 3 *pounds boneless pork or beef*
- *Water to cover*
- *Coarse salt*
- *Freshly ground pepper*
- 2 *medium onions, coarsely sliced*
- 2 *tablespoons dark brown sugar*
- 2 *fresh chilies, chopped*
- *Cinnamon stick*
- *A few cloves*
- *Dash thyme*
- 1 *tablespoon vinegar*
- 1 *tablespoon Worcestershire sauce*

The equivalent of our Sunday roast, this spicy stew is served with boiled potatoes or yams and often lasts families for a week, bits and pieces being added daily to keep the stew going.

• Simmer the chicken, pig's foot, and pork in water to cover for 1½ hours, skimming off any foam that may rise to the top. Add the remaining ingredients and cook for a further 30 minutes. Correct seasoning and serve. Serves 8.

SPICED LAMB SATÉ

- 2 *pounds boned lamb, cut in cubes*
- 2 *cloves garlic, minced*
- 2 *hot fresh chilies, minced, pages 27–29*
- 1 *teaspoon ground cumin*
- ½ *teaspoon ground allspice*
- ½ *teaspoon ground ginger*
- 1 *cup red wine vinegar*
- 4 *tablespoons brown sugar*
- 4 *tablespoons peanut oil*
- *Coarse salt and freshly ground pepper*

Serve with Indonesian Hot Pepper Relish, page 191, or Sambal Ketjap, page 190.

• Marinate the lamb in the garlic and spices at room temperature for an hour. Mix the remaining ingredients and pour onto the lamb. Leave for a couple of hours at room temperature or refrigerate overnight.

Thread the meat on oriental wooden skewers and grill over hot coals or under broiler until the meat is crisp and done according to your taste. Baste with the marinade. Serve with rice as a main course, accompanied by a sauce, or as an appetizer with sauce. Makes 8 skewers.

LAMB SATÉ

- 2 *pounds boneless lamb, cut in cubes*
- ¼ *cup ketjap manis, page 24, or dark soy sauce*
- 2 *cloves garlic, minced*
- *Juice of half a lemon*
- 1 *tablespoon minced fresh ginger*

This can be served as a main course with rice or as an appetizer. Indonesian Hot Pepper Relish, page 191, or Sambal Ketjap, page 190, are good with it.

• Marinate the lamb for a few hours at room temperature or refrigerated overnight in the remaining ingredients. Thread on small skewers (wooden oriental ones are the best) and broil over charcoal or under a grill until crisp, depending on how well done you like them. Serve with rice and sauce on the side or with sauce as an appetizer. Makes 8 skewers.

LAMB SATÉ IN MACADAMIA NUT SAUCE

- 2 *pounds boneless lamb, cubed*
- 2 *cloves garlic, minced*
- 2 *tablespoons dark soy sauce*
- *Coarse salt and freshly ground pepper*
- 1 *medium onion, finely chopped*
- 6 *Macadamia nuts, ground*
- 1 *fresh chili pepper, minced, pages 27–29*
- *Juice of half a lime or lemon*
- ½ *cup ketjap manis, page 24, or dark soy sauce*
- 2 *tablespoons brown sugar (omit if using ketjap manis)*

• Marinate the lamb for an hour at room temperature (or overnight refrigerated) in the garlic, soy sauce, salt, and pepper. Combine the remaining ingredients in a small saucepan with a little water and simmer for 20 minutes, or until onion is soft.

Thread the lamb on small skewers (wooden oriental ones are the best) and grill over hot coals or under a broiler until done according to your taste. Baste with the marinade. Serve the sauce separately. Makes 8 skewers.

PORK SATÉ

2 pound boneless pork butt
1 tablespoon ground coriander
1 medium onion, chopped
1 clove garlic, chopped
1 hot chili, chopped
1-inch piece of ginger, grated
3 tablespoons lime or lemon juice
Coarse salt to taste
2 tablespoon peanut or vegetable oil

Peanut Saté Sauce, page 181, Sambal Ketjap, page 190, or Indonesian Cucumber Relish, page 191, are the sauces and relishes that go best with this saté. Serve with white rice and a vegetable.

• Cut the pork into ¾-inch cubes. Combine the remaining ingredients except the oil in a blender and blend, adding a little water to make the mixture into a paste. Coat the pork cubes with the mixture and allow to marinate for several hours.

Thread the pork on skewers, brush with oil, and cook over hot coals or under a broiler. Makes 8 skewers.

PORK CHOPS CHARCUTIÈRE

4 thick pork chops
Flour
Coarse salt
Freshly ground pepper
4 tablespoons butter
4 tomatoes, peeled and chopped
½ cup water
1 tablespoon chopped shallots
¼ cup white wine
1 teaspoon vinegar
2 teaspoons mustard
2 tablespoons chopped pickles
1 tablespoon chopped parsley

Serve these with browned potatoes.

• Trim the pork chops, dredge them with seasoned flour, and fry them in 2 tablespoons butter for about 12–15 minutes on each side. Meanwhile, in a separate pan, cook the tomatoes in a tablespoon of butter with the water until you have a thick purée. Set aside.

When the chops are cooked, remove to a dish and keep warm. Melt the remaining butter in the frying pan and fry the shallots without browning. Add the white wine, vinegar, tomato purée, mustard, and pickles, and bring to a boil. Correct the seasoning, pour the mixture over the chops, sprinkle with parsley, and serve. Serves 4.

HUNGARIAN PORK CHOPS

- 4 *thick pork chops*
- 2 *tablespoons butter*
- *Dash olive oil*
- 1 *clove garlic, chopped*
- 1 *tablespoon Hungarian paprika*
- 1 *teaspoon marjoram*
- 1 *cup dry white wine*
- *Coarse salt and freshly ground pepper*

Noodles and a salad go with this simple dish.

• Trim the pork chops and wipe them dry with paper towels. In a casserole that will go both on top of and inside the stove, brown the chops in the butter and oil (oil is added to prevent the butter from burning). Remove the chops and sauté the garlic for a couple of minutes. Return the chops with the remaining ingredients and cook in a preheated 350-degree oven for about 45 minutes to an hour. Serves 4.

MANCHA MANTELES DE CERDO (PORK TABLECLOTH STAINER)

- 2 *pounds boneless pork, cubed*
- *Bay leaf*
- ½ *teaspoon oregano*
- ½ *teaspoon thyme*
- 4 *tomatoes, peeled*
- 3 *mulato chilies*
- 2 *ancho chilies*
- 1 *pasilla chili*
- 1 *medium onion, coarsely chopped*
- 4 *sprigs fresh coriander*
- 2 *garlic cloves, minced*
- ¼ *teaspoon powdered cloves*
- ¼ *teaspoon cinnamon*
- ½ *teaspoon cumin*
- 3 *tablespoons lard or salad oil*
- 2 *sweet potatoes, cooked and cubed*
- 2 *tart apples, sliced*
- 2 *large bananas, sliced*
- 1 *cup green peas*
- *Coarse salt and freshly ground pepper*

• Simmer the pork in water in a heavy casserole with the bay leaf, oregano, and thyme for 1½ hours. Meanwhile, prepare the chilies according to instructions on page 29.

Combine the tomatoes, chilies, onion, coriander, garlic, cloves, cinnamon, and cumin in a blender. Blend until smooth. Heat the lard in a large pan and add the mixture. Cook for 5 minutes, then stir in 1½ cups of the pork stock. Add the pork, remaining fruits and vegetables, salt and pepper to taste, and simmer for 30 minutes. Serves 4.

TEXAS CHILI CON CARNE

- 6 *pequín chilies, pages 27–29*
- 6 *ancho chilies, pages 27–29*
- 2 *pounds stewing beef, cut in ½-inch cubes*
- 1 *tablespoon olive oil*
- 2 *bay leaves*
- 1 *tablespoon cuminseed*
- 2 *cloves garlic, peeled*
- 2 *teaspoons oregano*
- 2 *tablespoons paprika*
- 1 *teaspoon sugar*
- *Coarse salt and freshly ground pepper*

Serve this with pinto beans and rice.

• Tear the chilies in strips and pour 2 cups of boiling water over them. Let soak for 30 minutes. Drain, reserving the liquid, and set aside. Heat the oil in a heavy skillet and brown the beef cubes. Add the chili-soaking liquid and bring to a boil. Add the bay leaves, turn down the heat, and let simmer for an hour. Meanwhile, purée the remaining ingredients, including the chilies, with a little water if needed, in an electric blender. Add the purée to the meat and let simmer for 30 minutes more. Serves 4.

AMERICAN INDIAN BARBECUED PORK ROAST

5½-pound pork roast

Sauce

- ½ *cup peanut or vegetable oil*
- 3 *medium onions, chopped*
- 3 *cloves garlic, chopped*
- 1 *teaspoon crushed coriander seed*
- 6 *juniper berries, crushed*
- 1 *bay leaf*
- 2 *pounds tomatoes*
- ¾ *cup tarragon vinegar*
- 1 *cup water*
- 1 *teaspoon crushed red chili pepper*
- 1 *tablespoon chili powder*
- *Coarse salt and freshly ground pepper*
- 1 *square unsweetened chocolate*

The resultant sauce from this roast is much like Mexican mole poblano sauce; the chocolate and the chilies give it a rich dark color. Rice, Fried Plantains, page 141, and a green vegetable would be good with it. So would Mexican Beans, page 151.

• In a saucepan heat the oil and sauté the onions with the garlic until soft. Add the remaining ingredients and simmer gently for 45 minutes, covered.

Arrange the trimmed roast in a roasting pan and bake in a preheated 350-degree oven for about 3½ hours, basting with the sauce. Serves 6.

TWICE-COOKED SZECHWAN PORK

- 1 *pound boneless pork*
- 3 *tablespoons peanut, vegetable, or sesame oil*
- 2 *cloves garlic, minced*
- 2 *tablespoons fresh ginger, chopped*
- 1 *leek, chopped*
- ½ *cup bamboo shoots*
- 1 *green bell pepper, chopped*
- ½ *teaspoon crushed Szechwan pepper*
- 1 *teaspoon sugar*
- 4 *tablespoons hoisin sauce*

• Simmer the pork (in one piece) in water to cover for 20 minutes. Remove, drain (reserving the liquid), and cut into pieces 1-inch square and ¼-inch thick. Heat the oil in a wok or skillet and stir-fry the pork cubes. Add the ginger, vegetables, and pepper. Stir-fry for 2–3 minutes. Add 2 tablespoons of the pork cooking liquid and remaining ingredients. Stir and cook for another minute. Remove and serve with plain white rice. Serves 2–4.

CHINESE PORK AND SHRIMP WITH PEPPERS

- 1 *pound boneless pork, diced*
- 3 *tablespoons soy sauce*
- 2 *tablespoons dry sherry*
- 1 *clove garlic, minced*
- 4 *tablespoons peanut, sesame, or vegetable oil*
- 3 *scallions, chopped (including green part)*
- 3 *bell peppers (red and green) chopped*
- 2 *hot fresh chilies, diced, pages 27–29*
- 2 *zucchini, cut in thin strips*
- 4 *large shrimp, peeled and cut in ¾-inch pieces*
- *Coarse salt and freshly ground black pepper*

• Marinate the pork in the soy sauce, sherry, and garlic for a couple of hours at room temperature (or overnight, refrigerated).

Drain the meat, reserving the marinade. Heat the oil in a skillet and stir-fry the meat for 3 minutes. Add the scallions, peppers, chilies, and zucchini, and stir-fry for 3 more minutes. Add the shrimp, stir-fry for 1 minute, stir in the marinade, season with salt and pepper, and serve with rice. Serves 3–4.

HUNGARIAN VEAL GOULASH

2 pounds stewing veal, cut into 1½-inch cubes
Flour
2 strips bacon, diced
2 tablespoons butter
3 medium onions, chopped
2 cloves garlic, chopped
2 tablespoons Hungarian paprika
1 tablespoon tomato purée
4 tomatoes, peeled and chopped, page 34
2 cups chicken stock
Coarse salt and freshly ground pepper
½ cup sour cream

Hungarian paprika is essential for this dish to be made properly.

• Dry the veal with paper towels and dredge with flour. Heat the bacon and butter in a heavy-bottomed casserole and brown the meat. Remove and drain. Add the onions and the garlic and cook until soft. Add the paprika, cook for a minute, then add tomato purée, tomatoes, and return meat to casserole. Season with salt and pepper. Pour in the stock and bring to a boil. Turn down heat and simmer gently for about 2 hours or until meat is tender. Before serving stir in sour cream, heat through, and correct seasoning. Serves 4–6.

BRITISH MUSTARD KIDNEYS

8 lamb or 4 veal kidneys (pork kidneys can also be used, but they are less delicate)
2 tablespoons Dijon-type mustard
4 tablespoons oil
2 tablespoons butter
2 shallots, chopped
½ cup dry white wine
Coarse salt and freshly ground pepper

Kidneys are a British staple. They are eaten at any time of day, particularly for breakfast—no Englishman would accept mixed-grill on the Brighton special were the kidneys missing. There is also a barbaric custom of serving kidneys as a savory at the end of a large dinner. Of course, kidneys should be eaten when they are very fresh and they should be lightly cooked so that they are pink in the middle. There is nothing like them.

• Trim the white filament from the inside of the kidneys, taking care not to damage them, with a pointed knife or nail scissors. Coat kidneys with a tablespoon of mustard and a couple of tablespoons of oil and let stand at room temperature for an hour or so.

Heat the remaining oil in a frying pan and quickly fry the kidneys, about 3 minutes on each side, and remove to a plate. Add the butter and fry the shallots without browning. Add the remaining mustard, the wine, and any juices that may have appeared on the plate with the kidneys. Season the sauce with salt and pepper, pour over the kidneys, and serve. Serves 4.

Note: These kidneys can also be grilled and the grilling pan then placed on top of the stove and the sauce made in it as above.

If more liquid is needed, a little veal or chicken stock may be used.

BRITISH DEVILLED KIDNEYS

- 4 *veal or* 8 *lamb kidneys*
- 2 *tablespoons chutney*
- 1 *tablespoon Dijon-type mustard*
- 1½ *tablespoons dry mustard*
- *Cayenne pepper to taste*
- *Oil*
- *Coarse salt and freshly ground pepper*

Serve these on toast for a light supper dish. Rice, a green vegetable, and grilled tomatoes would be typical British accompaniments.

• Remove the inside filament from the kidneys carefully, using a pointed knife or a pair of nail scissors. Wipe the kidneys with paper towels. In a bowl big enough to hold them, combine the chutney, mustards, and Cayenne, using the Cayenne according to how spicy you would like the kidneys to be. Let stand for a couple of hours at room temperature.

Put the kidneys in a broiling pan, preferably on a rack, brush with a little oil, and grill quickly under high heat, about 3 minutes on each side. Do not overcook or they will become tough. Scrape up the juices, season with salt and pepper, and pour them over the kidneys. Serves 4.

KIDNEYS WITH DEVILLED BUTTER

- *Devilled Butter, page* 193
- 4 *veal or* 8 *lamb kidneys*
- ½ *cup olive oil*
- 1 *teaspoon dry mustard*
- 1 *teaspoon powdered thyme*
- ½ *teaspoon ground mace*
- ¼ *teaspoon ground allspice*
- *Coarse salt and freshly ground pepper*

Green vegetables, grilled or baked tomatoes, and rice go well with this dish.

• Make the butter and refrigerate until ready for use. Trim the kidneys with a pointed knife, removing the white filament carefully, taking care not to cut up the kidney. Combine the oil, mustard, and spices and coat the kidneys with the mixture. Let stand at room temperature for 1 or 2 hours.

Put the kidneys on a broiling rack and broil under high heat for about 3 minutes on each side. Do not overcook or they will become tough. Remove to a heated plate, season with salt and pepper, and pour on any juices. Serve with a pat of the butter on each kidney or pass butter separately. Serves 4.

SAUSAGE GOULASH

- 3 *medium onions, chopped*
- ½ *stick butter*
- 1 *pound kielbasa*
- 2½ *pounds potatoes*
- 1½ *tablespoons paprika*
- *Coarse salt*
- *Freshly ground pepper*
- 1 *teaspoon marjoram*
- 1½ *cups water*

Use kielbasa (smoked sausage) for this recipe. If it is unavailable, other smoked sausage will do. Serve this with a green vegetable or a salad to follow. It is very filling.

• Soften the onions in the butter in a heavy casserole. Remove. Slice the sausage and sauté until brown. Cut the potatoes into 1-inch cubes and add to the casserole with the onions and remaining ingredients. Cook over low heat for about 30 minutes, or until potatoes are done. Uncover for last 10 minutes so that the sauce thickens. Serves 4.

LAPIN À LA MOUTARDE (MUSTARD RABBIT)

- 1 *rabbit*
- 2 *tablespoons Dijon-type mustard*
- 2 *tablespoons softened butter*
- 1 *tablespoon olive oil*
- 1 *cup dry white wine*
- *Coarse salt*
- *Freshly ground white pepper*
- 1 *cup fresh heavy cream*
- *Fresh chopped parsley*

Boiled rice is very good with this rabbit dish. Care must be taken to ensure that the rabbit is not allowed to dry out while cooking and that there is always plenty of sauce.

• Wipe the rabbit with paper towels, season the cavity, and coat with a mixture of the mustard, butter, and oil. Arrange in a casserole and pour in the white wine. Roast for about 45 minutes at 400 degrees, basting frequently. Season with salt and pepper and remove from casserole. Pour in the cream and over low heat on top of the stove scrape up the cooking juices. Pour into a sauceboat and pass separately, sprinkled with parsley. Serves 3–4.

CURRY

To many Westerners curry still means a fiery Indian sauce, deep yellow in color and thickened with flour, used indiscriminately with fish, meat, or chicken, accompanied by Major Grey's chutney and a mound of sticky rice. But the recent popularity of Indian restaurants and Indian specialty shops proves that many people are discovering the extraordinary variety of dishes that make up Indian and Pakistani cuisine. India and Pakistan cover a huge area; the food is radically different in each region. The United States must be the only country in the world where you can drive 500 miles and still find the same food at the end of your journey.

There are hundreds of curries, as many as there are stews in Western cooking. Each is made with different ingredients, and is different in flavor and hotness. Some are very delicate, some hot, and all obtain their flavors from ingenious use of spices. The rich color, the appetizing smell, the long slow cooking which produces a pungent, hot, or delicate sauce, the simple techniques—all combine to tempt people to try curries for themselves. They are marvelous for entertaining since they can be made the night before and improve the next day. Remember, though, that hot curries get even hotter as the flavors develop. Cold curries are also good and make excellent dishes for summer entertaining.

The word *curry* comes from the Indian word *kari*, which means sauce. In India this sauce is made from a mixture of spices prepared by the cook. Indians do not use all-purpose commercial powders. These are often made from the cheapest ingredients and have a harsh taste and a flatness about them which makes all curries taste alike.

Aromatics are the heart of Indian cooking. A good curry must be made with fresh home-ground spices. These should be stored in a cool place in a sealed container and away from light. Chilies and mustard seeds produce the heat in a curry. Cornstarch and flour are almost never used as thickening agents; turmeric and onions do that job. The juices from the meat or vegetables, yoghurt, or coconut milk also provide the sauce base and thickening. Tomatoes are not typical ingredients in an Indian curry; they tend sometimes to mask the other flavors and should be used with care. Depending on the browning of the meat, and on the spices and aromatics used, curries can be dark red or brown, green or light gold in color.

The basic "curry powder" is known as masala, and the proportions and balance of this masala are tremendously important. After trying a few combinations, most cooks settle on a mixture that suits their taste. And it's not so much which spices you use, but how you use them that makes a difference. Some spices are fried in ghee (clarified butter, see page 45) and added at the beginning; others are added toward the end. Cheap ingredients should never be used. You will waste your money because the results will be poor. Use fresh ingredients and experiment with ghee, or try using mustard oil or coconut oil. Meat cooked in mustard oil can be kept for weeks, according to Indian sources. All the spices used in curries are preservatives and have antiseptic value. For advice on grinding your own spices see the chapter on powders and pastes.

Madras curries are very hot and pungent; the sauce is quite thin. *Bengal* curries are cooked in mustard oil and served with rice. *Punjab* curries are eaten with lentils and flat, unleavened whole-wheat bread. *Bombay* food is cosmopolitan and the curries are highly spiced, using a lot of red-hot chilies. *Korma* curries are made with meat or vegetables braised with water or stock, yoghurt or cream. There are many different textures and tastes; the meat should be lean, and ghee, not oil, is used. *Kebab* curries are meat threaded on skewers and simmered in a spiced gravy. *Kofta* curries are meat or chicken balls cooked in a curry sauce, while *Keema* curries are made with ground meat. *Vindaloo* is a sour curry of meat or seafood marinated in a well-spiced vinegar marinade for several hours before cooking.

Curry should be accompanied by rice that is white and dry, with each grain separate. Saffron Rice, page 154, may also be used. See pages 153–154 for further information on cooking rice. The accompaniments should be arranged attractively in little dishes. Lentils (Dahl, page 159) and Indian breads may accompany curries. Try local Indian shops for ideas. For a small gathering or family meal, a curry dinner could consist of a main dish, a vegetable, rice, chutney, and yoghurt. For a large group, serve a meat curry, a fish curry, lentils, rice, two or three vegetable dishes, pickles, various chutneys, yoghurt, and salad.

The essential thing is to get the right balance of food. Serve a dry dish with a moist one, a bland curry with a fiery one, a chilled dish and a hot one, a sweet dish and a sour one, a preserved chutney and a fresh one.

Condiments for Curry

In addition to chutneys, pickles, and relishes, these condiments can be served with curry. Arrange them in little bowls on the table. If you are entertaining, keep extra condiments in the refrigerator in case you run out. Store them in plastic bags. If you don't need them at once, they will come in handy for other dishes later.

Sliced bananas with lemon juice squeezed on them
Chopped apples with lemon juice
Chopped peanuts
Chopped tomatoes
Chopped onion
Sliced cucumbers
Yoghurt, page 46
Grated coconut
Chopped parsley
Chopped chives
Chopped scallions
Raisins
Chopped hardboiled eggs

WHOLE EGG CURRY

12 hardboiled eggs
¼ pound slivered almonds
1 tablespoon ground saffron
¼ tablespoon turmeric
4 tablespoons lime juice
1 tablespoon ground chili peppers
1 tablespoon garlic salt
1 bay leaf, ground
2 cups plain yoghurt
½ cup heavy cream
½ cup chicken stock (more or less as necessary)
Coarse salt and freshly ground pepper
1 tablespoon roasted sesame seeds
Chopped chives to garnish

This is an attractive dish for a party. Serve it with rice, chutney, and condiments. It improves if made the day before.

• Peel the eggs and stick them all over with almond slivers. Make gashes down to the yolk, but not right through. Combine the saffron, turmeric, lime juice, chili peppers, garlic salt, and bay leaf. Coat the eggs with this mixture.

In a large saucepan heat the yoghurt and the cream and add the eggs. Season with salt and pepper, bring to a boil, and simmer over medium heat, adding stock if necessary, until sauce is thick. Sprinkle with sesame seeds and chives, and serve. Serves 6–8.

BANANA CURRY

- 1½ *pounds bananas*
- 1 *tablespoon ghee,* *page* 45, *or butter*
- ½ *teaspoon turmeric*
- 1 *teaspoon caraway seeds*
- ½ *teaspoon ground chili*
- ¼ *cup yoghurt*
- ½ *teaspoon Garam Masala,* *page* 40
- *Juice of half a lemon*
- *Coarse salt*

This is a side dish and goes well with large curry dinners. Use slightly underripe bananas.

• Slice the bananas and squeeze a little lemon juice on them to prevent them from turning brown. Heat the ghee and add the turmeric and caraway seeds. Fry for a couple of minutes, then add the bananas with the chili. Cook for about 5 minutes, then add remaining ingredients and cook for 10 minutes. Serves 4.

VEGETABLE CURRY

- 4 *tablespoons peanut or vegetable oil*
- 4 *medium onions, sliced*
- 4 *cloves garlic, chopped*
- ½ *tablespoon chili powder*
- 2 *tablespoons Mild Curry Powder,* *page* 40
- ½ *tablespoon turmeric*
- ½ *tablespoon coriander seeds*
- 1 *bay leaf*
- 6 *cloves*
- ½ *teaspoon cinnamon*
- 1 *teaspoon sugar*
- 6 *tomatoes, chopped*
- 6 *carrots, chopped*
- 4 *small turnips, diced (or* 2 *large ones)*
- 2 *pounds potatoes, diced*
- 2 *beets, diced*
- 6 *stalks celery with leaves, chopped*
- 2 *cups lentils*
- *Water or stock to cover*
- *Coarse salt and freshly ground black pepper*
- 1 *can chick peas*
- 1 *package frozen green beans*

This can be served on its own or with a meat or egg curry.

• Heat the oil in a large pot. Soften the onions with the garlic and add the chili powder, curry powder, turmeric, coriander seeds, and bay leaf. Cook, stirring, for 3 minutes. Add the cloves, cinnamon, sugar, and tomatoes. Cook for another 2 minutes. Add the remaining ingredients except the chick peas and green beans. Simmer gently for about an hour, or until the potatoes, lentils, and carrots are cooked. Put in more water if curry seems too dry. Add the beans and peas, heat through, season with salt and pepper, and serve. Serves 8–10.

POTATO CURRY

- 1 *medium onion, chopped*
- 1 *tablespoon ghee, page 45, or butter*
- 2 *tablespoons chopped fresh coriander or parsley*
- 1 *teaspoon turmeric*
- ½ *teaspoon chili powder*
- *Coarse salt*
- 1 *pound potatoes, cut small*
- 1 *teaspoon Garam Masala, page 40*
- *Juice of half a lemon*

This is very good with new potatoes. Serve as a vegetable or with curry. If you are cooking for a large number of people, this curry makes a good side dish.

• Fry the onion in the ghee until golden. Add the coriander, turmeric, chili powder, and salt, and fry for a few minutes. Add the potatoes and a little water. Cook over low heat for about 30 minutes. For the last 10 minutes of cooking time add the masala and lemon juice. Serves 4.

SIMPLE CHICKEN CURRY

- 1 *3–4-pound frying chicken, cut up*
- 2 *tablespoons ghee, page 45, or butter*
- 2 *medium onions, chopped*
- 2 *cloves garlic, chopped*
- 2 *teaspoons Garam Masala, page 40*
- *Water or stock to cover*
- *Coarse salt and freshly ground pepper*

Serve with rice and condiments suggested on page 129.

• Dry the chicken pieces with paper towels. Heat the ghee in a heavy-bottomed casserole and fry the chicken until golden. Remove and set aside. Soften the onions and garlic in the ghee. Add the masala and cook, stirring, for 2 minutes, taking care to prevent burning. Add the stock or water, season with salt and pepper, and return the chicken to the casserole. Simmer gently until chicken is done, about 30–45 minutes. Serves 4.

TRINIDAD SHRIMP CURRY

- 2 *pounds large shrimp*
- 1½ *teaspoons cumin*
- 1½ *teaspoons coriander*
- 1½ *teaspoons mustard seeds*
- 1½ *teaspoons peppercorns*
- 1½ *teaspoons turmeric*
- ½ *teaspoon crushed red hot pepper*
- 1 *bay leaf*
- 4 *tablespoons ghee, page 45, or 2 tablespoons peanut oil and 2 tablespoons butter*
- 2 *onions, finely chopped*
- 2 *cloves garlic, minced*
- 1 *tablespoon chopped fresh ginger*
- 4 *tomatoes, peeled and chopped, page 34*
- *Coarse salt and freshly ground pepper*
- *Juice of 1 lime*
- *Water as necessary*

Serve with boiled rice and Green Mango Chutney, page 188.

• Shell the shrimp and devein them. Combine the spices in an electric grinder or pound together using a pestle and mortar. In a large, heavy skillet heat the ghee. Fry the onions with the garlic and ginger without browning. Add the ground spices and cook for 3 minutes, taking care not to burn the mixture. Add the tomatoes and lime juice, season with salt and pepper, and simmer gently for 30 minutes, adding water if the sauce becomes dry.

Add the shrimp and coat them with the sauce. Cook, covered, for 5 minutes. Be careful not to overcook them, they should be juicy and pink. Serve immediately. Serves 4.

BHUNA CHICKEN

- 1 *3–3½-pound chicken, skinned and cut up*
- 1 *medium onion, chopped*
- 2 *cloves garlic, finely chopped*
- 2 *tablespoons ghee, page 45, or butter*
- 1 *teaspoon turmeric*
- 2 *teaspoons Garam Masala, page 40*
- 1 *teaspoon chili powder*
- 3 *tomatoes, peeled and chopped*
- 1 *tablespoon lemon juice*
- 1 *tablespoon grated coconut*
- *Coarse salt*
- *Fresh chopped coriander to garnish*

This is a "dry" curry, meaning that it is cooked without stock or other liquid. Cook it over very low heat, preferably on a trivet. Serve it with rice.

• Dry the chicken with paper towels. Fry the onion with the garlic in the ghee until golden. Add the remaining ingredients (except coriander), turning the chicken so that it is thoroughly coated with the spices. Cover tightly and cook over very low heat for about 1 hour. Sprinkle with coriander. Serves 4.

THAI CHICKEN CURRY

- 3 *cups Coconut Milk, page* 44
- 2 *tablespoons Thai Curry Paste, page* 41
- 4 *chicken breasts, boned and cut into inch-long strips*
- 2 *tablespoons bottled fish sauce, page* 24
- *Chopped fresh basil to garnish*
- 2 *chopped fresh red or green chilies*
- *Coarse salt*

Use either red or green paste for this curry. Prepare the coconut milk in advance. Serve the curry with rice and a sambal.

• Bring 1 cup coconut milk to a boil. Add the paste and simmer for about 5 minutes. Add the chicken, the remaining coconut milk, and fish sauce, and simmer for about 15 minutes, until the chicken is cooked and the sauce has reduced. Season with salt, sprinkle with basil and chilies. Serves 4.

CHICKEN KORMA

good

- 2 2½-*pound chickens, cut up*
- 2 *cups yoghurt*
- 3 *cloves garlic, chopped*
- 2 *medium onions, chopped*
- 1 *teaspoon paprika*
- 2 *teaspoons fresh ginger, finely chopped*
- *Coarse salt and freshly ground pepper to taste*
- 4 *tablespoons butter or ghee, page* 45
- 3 *teaspoons ground coriander*
- ½ *teaspoon ground chili*
- 2 *teaspoons cumin*
- 2 *cardomom seeds*
- 1 *teaspoon poppy seeds*
- 1 *tablespoon turmeric*
- 1 *bay leaf*
- 2 *tablespoons chopped fresh mint leaves (optional)*

• Place the chicken in a bowl and marinate for a few hours in the yoghurt, 1 clove garlic, half an onion, paprika, ginger, salt, and pepper.

Melt the butter in a large heavy pan and fry the remaining onions and garlic until golden. Remove, and add the coriander, chili, cumin, poppy seeds, and turmeric. Fry for a few minutes. Add the chicken pieces, sear, and then pour in enough water to cover and any remaining marinade. Return the onions and garlic, bay leaf and mint, and simmer for about 45 minutes, or until chicken is tender. Serves 6.

KOFTA CURRY

Meatballs

- 1 *medium onion, finely chopped*
- 2 *cloves garlic, finely chopped*
- ½ *green bell pepper, finely chopped*
- 1 *tablespoon ghee, page 45, or butter*
- 2 *tablespoons fresh coriander or parsley, chopped*
- *Coarse salt and freshly ground pepper*
- 1½ *pounds ground meat (beef, lamb, or pork)*
- 1 *tablespoon Garam Masala, page 40*
- ½ *tablespoon chili powder*
- 1 *egg*
- *Oil for deep frying*

Curry Sauce

- 1 *medium onion, chopped*
- *1-inch piece ginger, chopped*
- 1 *tablespoon ghee, page 45, or butter*
- 1 *teaspoon turmeric*
- ½ *teaspoon chili powder*
- ½ *teaspoon Garam Masala, page 40*
- 1½ *pounds tomatoes, peeled and chopped*
- *Stock to cover*

Koftas are little meatballs and make a good, economical curry. Serve the curry with rice and a fresh chutney. You may also make the meatballs without the sauce, and serve them on toothpicks as an hors d'oeuvre, using the chutney as a dip.

• Soften the onion with the garlic and pepper in the ghee. Combine in a bowl with the remaining ingredients for meatballs, except the oil. Form into balls (golf-ball size) and fry in oil until brown.

Meanwhile make the curry sauce. Soften the onion with the ginger in the ghee. Add the spices, cook for a couple of minutes, then add the tomatoes and a little stock. Bring to a boil and when thickened slightly add the meatballs with more stock to cover if necessary. Heat through and serve. Serves 4.

KEEMA CURRY

1 tablespoon ghee, page 45, or butter
1 medium onion, chopped
2 cloves garlic, chopped
2 tablespoons fresh coriander or parsley, chopped
1 pound ground beef
1 teaspoon turmeric
½ teaspoon chili powder
4 tomatoes, peeled and chopped
Coarse salt
1 tablespoon Garam Masala, page 40
1 cup peas

The curry will be much improved if you mince your own meat with a meat grinder. Serve this curry with Chapattis, page 157, and rice.

• Heat the ghee and fry the onion with the garlic until golden. Add the coriander, meat, turmeric, and chili powder. Bring to a boil, add tomatoes, salt, and cook over very low heat (on an asbestos mat if possible) for 30 minutes. Add the garam masala and the peas. Cook for another 15–20 minutes. Serves 4.

EAST AFRICAN BEEF AND BANANA CURRY

4 bananas or plantains
1½ pounds boneless beef, cubed
3 tablespoons olive oil or ghee, page 45
2 medium onions, chopped
2 carrots, sliced
1 leek, chopped
3 cloves garlic, minced
¾ teaspoon turmeric
1 teaspoon ground chili
½ teaspoon cumin
½ teaspoon ground coriander
½ teaspoon caraway seeds
1 cinnamon stick
½ teaspoon ground ginger
1½ tablespoons flour
1½ cups tomato purée
Coarse salt and freshly ground pepper
½ cup red wine

• Slice the plantains and simmer for 15 minutes in boiling water. If using bananas do not boil them. Brown the beef in the oil, add the onions, carrots, leeks, and garlic. Fry until golden, add the spices, cook for 2 minutes, then add the flour. Cook for 2 or 3 minutes, taking care to prevent burning. Add the tomato purée, salt, pepper, and wine, and bring to a boil. Simmer for 25 minutes. Add water if curry seems dry. Add the bananas and simmer for 25 minutes. Serves 4.

BEEF VINDALOO

- 1½ *pounds boneless beef*
- 2–3 *tablespoons Indian Vindaloo Paste, page 42*
- 3 *tablespoons ghee, page 45*
- *Water*
- *Coarse salt*

A hot, spicy, sweet-sour curry, serve this with white rice and chutney. If possible leave the meat overnight in the paste and leave it again for another night once it has been cooked.

• Cut the beef into 1½-inch cubes and pat dry with paper towels. Put the meat in a large bowl and toss thoroughly to coat with the paste. Allow to marinate for at least 4 hours.

Melt the ghee in a heavy casserole. Fry the beef carefully to prevent burning it, and add enough water to make a gravy. Season with salt. Cover and cook over low heat for about 1½ hours or until the meat is tender. Serves 4.

SIMPLE LAMB BIRYANI

- 2 *pounds boneless lamb*
- 1 *teaspoon ground coriander*
- ½ *teaspoon ground cloves*
- ½ *teaspoon ground cardamom*
- ¼ *teaspoon ground chili*
- ½ *teaspoon ground cumin*
- ½ *teaspoon ground cinnamon*
- *Coarse salt*
- *Freshly ground pepper*
- *1-inch piece fresh ginger, chopped*
- 3 *cloves garlic, chopped*
- *Juice of 1 lemon*
- 2 *cups yoghurt*
- 2 *medium onions*
- 2 *tablespoons ghee, page 45, or butter*
- 3 *cups Patna rice, cooked, page 153*

A popular Moslem dish, serve this with chutney.

• Cut the lamb into cubes and marinate for a few hours in a mixture of the spices, ginger, garlic, lemon juice, and yoghurt. Fry the onions in the ghee until soft, add the lamb and a little water to make a gravy for the lamb to cook in. Cover, and cook over low heat until done (about 1½ hours).

In a heavy casserole layer alternately the rice and the lamb, finishing with the rice. Bake in a low oven for half an hour. Serves 4.

VEGETABLES

In many countries where hot food is eaten, people are either vegetarian or eat very little meat. As a result, countless interesting recipes for vegetables cooked with hot spices have been developed. Some of the vegetable dishes in this chapter are good as side dishes in buffets. Two or three can be combined and served as a main course, accompanied perhaps by white rice and a couple or relishes or table sauces.

Vegetables should not be cooked in large amounts of boiling water. Unless they are cooked in the sauce in which they are to be served, they should be steamed. They should be bright in color, crisp, and fresh. Steaming preserves the vitamins and minerals that would dissolve in water.

FRIED RIPE PLANTAINS OR BANANAS

Plantains or bananas
Lemon or lime juice
Peanut oil

These are delicious with Mexican or Caribbean dishes. Use greenish bananas if you cannot get ripe plantains. Overripe bananas will not hold their shape.

• Peel and slice the bananas (lengthwise or in rounds, according to your preference—and the size of the plantains) and squeeze lemon juice over them. Heat enough oil to cover the bottom of a heavy skillet and fry until golden brown. Season with coarse salt and serve immediately.

MEXICAN STRING BEANS WITH CHILIES

1 *tablespoon peanut, vegetable, or olive oil*
1 *medium onion, chopped*
1 *clove garlic, chopped (optional)*
2 *chilies, chopped*
2 *tomatoes, peeled and chopped*
1 *pound string beans*
¾ *cup boiling water*
Coarse salt to taste

An excellent way to cook the rather large string beans that are available fresh in the market. These beans go very well with lamb or pork chops, fried, grilled, or roast chicken, or grilled fish.

Use fresh green or red chilies if available; if not, use canned chilies.

• Heat the oil in a skillet and gently fry the onion with the garlic without browning. Add the chilies and fry for a couple of minutes. Add the tomatoes, the beans, and the water, bring to a boil, cover, and turn down the heat. Let the beans simmer gently until they are done (about 15 minutes), adding a little more water if you need it. Remove from heat, season with salt, and serve. Serves 4.

STIR-FRIED SPICED CABBAGE

- 1 *pound Chinese cabbage (or green cabbage)*
- 2 *tablespoons sugar*
- 2 *tablespoons vinegar*
- 1 *tablespoon soy sauce*
- ¼–½ *teaspoon Cayenne pepper*
- *Coarse salt*
- 1 *tablespoon peanut, vegetable, or sesame oil*
- 2 *cloves garlic, minced*
- 3 *scallions, chopped (including green part)*

• Slice the cabbage fine. In a bowl, combine the sugar, vinegar, soy sauce, Cayenne, and salt.

Heat the oil in a large skillet or wok. Add the garlic and scallions and stir-fry for 2 minutes. Add the cabbage and stir-fry for 2–3 minutes. Stir in the vinegar mixture, heat through, and remove from flame. Cool and serve at room temperature. Serves 4.

CHILES RELLENOS

These stuffed peppers are made with poblano chilies, which are slightly smaller, darker, and much hotter than green peppers. The latter can be substituted but the taste is not the same at all.

The chilies should be held with a fork over a gas flame until the skin is charred and blistered. Wrap them in a dish towel and let stand for a few minutes. Peel the skin, slit them along the side, and remove the veins and seeds. If you use bell peppers, slice the top off and use it as a lid. Stuff the chilies with the stuffing mixture (see below) and secure the opening with a toothpick. You are then ready to dip them into the batter and fry them in hot oil.

Chilies Stuffed with Cheese

Place a slice of Monterey Jack or mozzarella cheese inside each chili. Separate 2 eggs. Dust the chilies with flour, then dip them into the beaten eggs yolks, then the stiffly beaten egg whites. Fry the chilies in hot lard or peanut oil until golden brown. Put in casserole dish and bake in a hot oven for 20 minutes covered with Mexican Tomato Sauce, page 178.

Chilies Stuffed with Beans

Stuff the chilies with approximately ½ cup Mexican Refried Beans, page 150, for each chili. Dip into batter and fry as suggested in preceding recipe. Place in casserole, cover with heavy cream and grated Cheddar cheese. Bake for about 20 minutes in a hot oven.

CAULIFLOWER CHILI

1 *whole cauliflower*
Water

Sauce
1 *tablespoon peanut or vegetable oil*
1 *medium onion, chopped*
2 *cloves garlic, chopped*
1 *tablespoon Homemade Chili Powder, page 42*
3 *tomatoes, peeled and chopped*
½ *teaspoon ground cloves*
Dash cinnamon
Coarse salt and freshly ground pepper to taste

½ *cup grated Cheddar cheese*
2 *tablespoons breadcrumbs or wheat germ*
Fresh chopped parsley to garnish

Serve this cauliflower with grilled meat or chicken and Mexican Beans, page 151.

• Bring about an inch of water to a rolling boil and cook the cauliflower, covered, for about 10 minutes. Drain and reserve the water.

Heat the oil in a skillet and fry the onion with the garlic until soft. Add the chili powder, tomatoes, cloves, cinnamon, salt, and pepper. Cook together for about 5 minutes. Moisten with cauliflower water as necessary. Arrange the cauliflower in a greased baking dish and spoon the sauce over it. Sprinkle with cheese and breadcrumbs and bake in a preheated 350-degree oven for about 30 minutes. Sprinkle with parsley and serve. Serves 6.

OKRA WITH CHILI AND CUMIN

- 1 *pound okra*
- 3 *tablespoons ghee, page* 45, *or butter*
- 1 *medium onion, finely chopped*
- 1 *tablespoon ground cumin*
- 1 *tablespoon ground chili*
- *Coarse salt*

This is an Indian dish. Serve it along with rice with chicken, lamb, or fish dishes, or with curry.

• Trim the ends off the okra and wash. Heat the ghee in a skillet and gently fry the onion until golden without browning. Add the cumin and chili and fry for another minute. Pour in a little water, just enough to cover the bottom of the pan. Add okra and salt. Cover and cook over medium heat, stirring frequently, for about 20 minutes. Serves 4.

DEVILLED TOMATOES

- 4 *tomatoes, halved*
- 1 *clove garlic, finely chopped*
- *Coarse salt*
- *Freshly ground pepper*
- *Cayenne pepper*
- *Breadcrumbs*
- *Olive oil*
- 2 *tablespoons butter*
- 1 *teaspoon Dijon-type mustard*
- *Dash Worcestershire sauce*
- *Dash Tabasco sauce*
- 1 *tablespoon red wine vinegar*
- 1 *teaspoon sugar*
- *Fresh chopped parsley*

Serve with steaks and grilled meat or seafood.

• Arrange the tomatoes on a broiling pan and sprinkle with garlic, salt, pepper, Cayenne, breadcrumbs, and olive oil. Broil.

Meanwhile, in a small saucepan combine the remaining ingredients except the parsley. Bring to a boil and set aside. Arrange the tomatoes on a dish and put a little sauce on each one. Sprinkle with parsley and serve. Serves 4.

FRIED GREEN TOMATOES

- 2 *pounds green tomatoes*
- 1 *teaspoon Tabasco sauce*
- 1 *teaspoon soy sauce*
- 1 *teaspoon Worcestershire sauce*
- 1 *cup flour*
- 1 *teaspoon Cayenne pepper*
- ½ *teaspoon chili powder*
- ¼ *teaspoon powdered mustard*
- ¼ *teaspoon cumin*
- *Coarse salt and freshly ground pepper*
- *Peanut or olive oil for frying*

These are delicious with chicken, pork, or mackerel.

• Slice the tomatoes and marinate them in a mixture of Tabasco, soy sauce, and Worcestershire sauce for half an hour. Combine the remaining ingredients except the oil in a large bowl or plastic bag and coat the tomato slices. Heat enough oil to cover the bottom of a frying pan and fry the tomatoes until brown and crisp. Serve at once. Serves 4.

BALKAN MUSHROOMS WITH BLACK PEPPER

- 2 *pounds mushrooms*
- 1 *medium onion, chopped*
- 4 *tablespoons butter*
- 1 *tablespoon freshly ground pepper*
- *Coarse salt to taste*
- 1 *tablespoon fresh chopped dill*
- ½ *cup sour cream*

Serve these mushrooms with noodles and a meat dish.

• Slice the mushrooms. Soften onion in the butter in a frying pan and add the mushrooms. Grind on the pepper and add the salt and dill. Cook until the mushrooms are done, then add the cream. Heat through (do not boil) and serve. Serves 4.

PAPRIKA ONIONS WITH YOGHURT

- 4 *large onions*
- 1 *stick butter*
- *Dash olive oil*
- ¼ *teaspoon mace*
- ¼ *teaspoon freshly grated nutmeg*
- 1 *tablespoon Hungarian paprika*
- ½ *tablespoon flour*
- 1 *cup plain yoghurt*
- *Coarse salt and freshly ground black pepper*

A Balkan dish, this goes well with pork, veal, or chicken, accompanied by noodles.

• Slice the onions and fry them in the butter with the oil, mace, nutmeg, and paprika until they are soft but not brown. Sprinkle on the flour and cook for 2 or 3 minutes, stirring. Add the yoghurt, stir well, and heat through. Correct seasoning and serve. Serves 4.

INDIAN SPICED EGGPLANT

- 1 *large eggplant*
- *Coarse salt*
- 4 *tablespoons ghee, page* 45, *or butter*
- 1½ *tablespoons ground coriander*
- *Freshly ground pepper*
- 2 *tablespoons sesame seeds*
- 1 *teaspoon paprika*
- *Pinch asafœtida*
- *1-inch piece fresh ginger, chopped*
- *Juice of 1 lime or lemon*
- 2 *tablespoons chopped coriander to garnish*
- 1 *tablespoon chopped chives to garnish*

You can serve this with an Indian meal or with grilled meats such as lamb or chicken. It is an unusual, slightly sweet-sour dish and very good—one of the best ways I've eaten eggplant.

• Slice the eggplant, salt it, and let it stand for an hour. Heat 2 tablespoons ghee and fry the slices quickly on both sides. You may find that the eggplant soaks up the ghee—if so, add a little more, but not much or the dish will be too greasy. Simply dry-fry the slices to brown them. Set the eggplant aside. Fry the spices and ginger in remaining ghee and add the eggplant. Add the lime juice and cover. Simmer over very low heat until done, sprinkle with coriander and chives, and serve. Serves 6.

STARCH DISHES

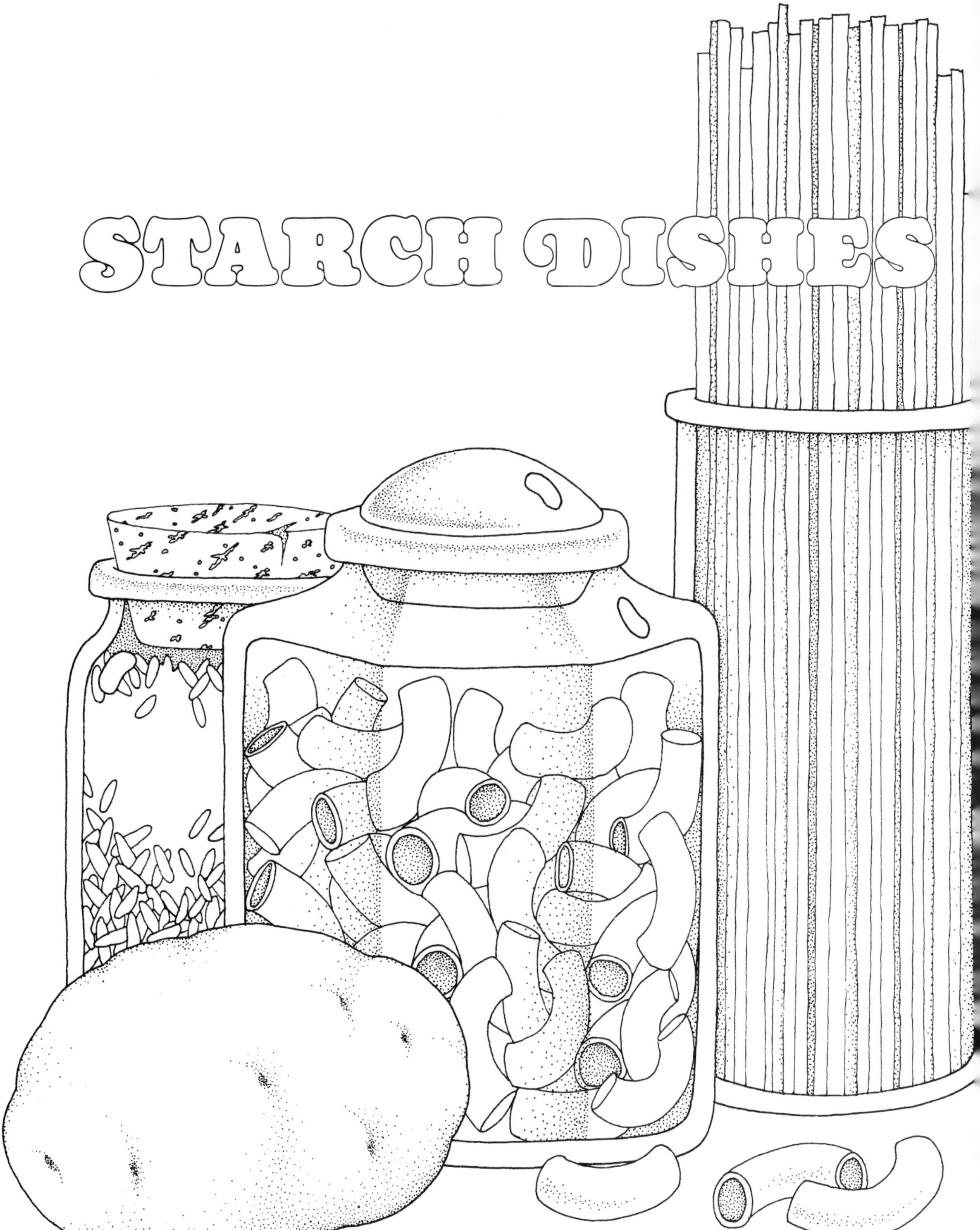

The recipes in this chapter are mainly accompaniments to spicy food. Each cuisine has its own particular way of cooking rice, noodles, beans, or potatoes and various kinds of breads to serve with a main course. Many of the dishes made from these ingredients are unusual and colorful—rice cooked with tomatoes and peppers, potatoes served with chilies and a cream sauce, beans and bananas mashed in a pancake, red and green enchiladas, and black beans combined with white rice, to name a few.

ENCHILADAS

Enchiladas are tortillas dipped in sauce, stuffed, rolled, and baked in the oven. They make excellent lunch dishes. You can stuff them with a variety of mixtures: cheese, cooked plantains, leftover meat or chicken, sausage. They are also very good with a mole sauce (see recipe for Turkey Mole Poblano, page 105).

Red Enchiladas

- 6 *ancho chilies, soaked in boiling water for 30 minutes, pages 27–29*
- 4 *tomatoes, peeled and chopped, page 34*
- 2 *medium onions, finely chopped*
- 2 *cloves garlic, chopped*
- *Sprig of epazote, if available*
- ½ *teaspoon sugar*
- *Coarse salt and freshly ground black pepper*
- 2 *eggs, lightly beaten*
- 1 *cup heavy cream*
- *Lard or peanut oil*
- 6 *chorizos, skinned and chopped*
- ½ *cup freshly grated Parmesan or Cheddar cheese*
- 12 *tortillas*

Ground meat (see also Picadillo, page 111) or Italian hot sausage can be used instead of the chorizos.

• Combine the chilies, tomatoes, 1 chopped onion, garlic, sugar, salt, and pepper in a blender. Moisten with some of the chili-soaking liquid. Blend at high speed to a smooth purée. Mix eggs with cream. Heat 2 tablespoons lard or oil in a heavy skillet. Add the chili-tomato mixture and cook for 5 minutes, stirring. Remove from heat, slowly stir in the egg-and-cream mixture. Set aside.

In another skillet fry the sausage meat and remove with slotted spoon. Add more lard or fat. Dip the tortillas into the sauce, then fry them very lightly in the fat, just enough to soften them. Don't fry too long or they will become hard. In each tortilla place a spoonful of the sausage meat. Roll them up and put them in an ovenproof dish. When you have filled the dish with the enchiladas, pour on the rest of the sauce and sprinkle with remaining chopped onion and grated cheese. Bake in a hot oven for about 15 minutes. Serves 6.

Green Enchiladas

very good

- 6 *poblano chilies, skinned and chopped, pages 27–29*
- 1 *10-ounce can Mexican green tomatoes*
- ¼ *cup coarsely chopped fresh coriander*
- *Coarse salt and freshly ground pepper*
- 2 *eggs, lightly beaten*
- 1 *cup heavy cream*
- 12 *tortillas*
- 3 *tablespoons lard or peanut oil*
- 3 *whole chicken breasts, cooked and diced*
- 6 *ounces cream cheese*
- 1 *medium onion, finely chopped*
- ¼ *cup freshly grated Parmesan cheese*

• Combine the chilies, green tomatoes, coriander, and salt and pepper in a blender with enough liquid from the tomatoes to make a thick purée. Mix eggs with the cream and add to the purée. Combine chicken and cream cheese and moisten with some of the sauce.

Dip the tortillas into the purée and fry in the lard as in preceding recipe. Spread with chicken mixture, roll up, and place in ovenproof dish. Bring remaining sauce to a boil, pour over enchiladas, sprinkle with cheese and onions, and bake for about 15 minutes in a hot oven. Serves 6.

MEXICAN REFRIED BEANS

- ½ *recipe Mexican Beans*
- *Lard, bacon fat, or peanut oil*

• Cook the beans according to Mexican Beans, page 151. Canned beans may be used. They improve if you fry an onion, a garlic clove, and a chopped chili in the fat and mash them into the beans.

Mash the beans well with a fork. Heat the fat in a skillet. Add the beans and mash them in, stirring continuously. If you like, add some ground cumin, oregano, or crushed garlic. More fat, more mashing, and when they are hot and sizzling and have become crisp underneath, turn them out and serve them. Serves 4.

MEXICAN BEANS

- 1 *pound dried beans*
- *Water to cover*
- 1 *medium onion, coarsely chopped*
- *Bay leaf*
- *Coarse salt and freshly ground black pepper*
- 1 *small green fresh chili chopped fine, pages 27–29*
- *Herb bouquet (parsley and thyme, tied in cheesecloth)*

Mexicans don't usually bother to soak the beans overnight. They leave them to simmer at the back of the stove until they are cooked, adding more water as needed and skimming off any foam that rises to the top. Beans accompany almost every meal and come in a variety of colors and sizes. The most common are *frijol negro* (black bean), *frijol pinto* (pinto bean), *frijol rojo* (kidney and California pink bean), and *frijol canario* (pale yellow bean).

Beans are particularly good with pork, spareribs, chicken, accompanied by fried bananas. They should be fairly soupy. Do not use stale beans, they take almost forever to cook.

• Cover the beans with water in a large, heavy-bottomed casserole. Add the remaining ingredients and simmer, partially covered, until cooked, adding more water as needed. Serves 4.

SERBIAN BEANS

- 1 *pound navy beans, soaked in water overnight*
- 3 *medium onions, coarsely chopped*
- ½ *pound smoked ham, cut into 1-inch cubes*
- *Coarse salt and freshly ground pepper*
- 1 *tablespoon butter*
- 1 *tablespoon Hungarian paprika*

Serve these beans with Sausage Goulash, page 124, or with salad.

• Drain the beans and simmer in water to cover with 2 of the onions, the ham, and salt and pepper for about 2 hours. Fry the remaining onion in the butter and add the paprika. Cook for a minute and add to the beans. Cook for 10 minutes. Correct seasoning and serve. Serves 4.

YUGOSLAV PAPRIKA POTATOES

- 2 *pounds potatoes*
- 2 *medium onions*
- 1 *tablespoon peanut or vegetable oil*
- 2 *tablespoons butter*
- 2 *tablespoons Hungarian paprika*
- ½ *cup sour cream*
- *Coarse salt to taste*
- *Pimiento strips and chopped parsley to garnish*

Serve these with chicken, pork or veal chops, steak or a roast. The only other vegetable you will need is a green salad.

• Boil the potatoes until done. Meanwhile, chop the onions and fry gently until soft in the oil and butter. Add the paprika and continue cooking for 2 minutes, being careful to prevent burning. Set aside.

Mash the potatoes and mix in the onions and the sour cream. Season with salt and put the mixture in a buttered baking dish. Dot with butter and a little paprika and brown under a broiler. Garnish with pimiento and parsley and serve. Serves 4.

PERUVIAN SWEET POTATOES

- 6 *sweet potatoes, baked in their skins*
- 4 *ounces cream cheese*
- 1 *egg yolk*
- 1 *teaspoon chili powder*
- 3 *scallions, chopped*
- *Coarse salt and freshly ground pepper to taste*
- *Butter*

These baked potatoes are excellent with pork chops or spareribs, turkey, or chicken. A green vegetable would be a good accompaniment.

• Mash the flesh from the sweet potatoes, reserving the skins. Add the remaining ingredients except the butter and stuff back into the skins. Dot with butter, sprinkle with extra chili powder, and quickly brown on a hot grill, or under a broiler. Serves 6.

JAVANESE POTATOES WITH TAMARIND SAUCE

- 1 *red or green bell pepper, chopped*
- 1 *medium onion, chopped*
- 1 *clove garlic, chopped*
- 2 *tablespoons peanut or vegetable oil*
- ½ *cup Tamarind Water, page 45*
- 1 *tablespoon dark brown sugar*
- ½ *inch ginger, chopped*
- ¼ *teaspoon trassi (shrimp paste), page 24*
- *Coarse salt*
- 4 *medium-size potatoes*
- *Oil for deep-frying*

Prepared in advance, the potatoes can be kept hot in the oven in their sauce. Serve them with other Indonesian and Southeast Asian dishes, or with chicken or meat.

• Fry the pepper, onion, and garlic in the peanut oil until soft. Add the tamarind water, dark brown sugar, and ginger. Mix well, add the trassi and salt. Bring to a boil and simmer until the liquid has reduced to a thick paste. Set aside.

Cut the potatoes into thin slices and deep-fry until golden. Drain on paper towels. Combine with the sauce and serve hot. Serves 4.

INDIAN POTATO FRITTERS

1 cup mashed potatoes
3 eggs
1 finely minced green chili
2 tablespoons chopped onion or scallion
2 tablespoons milk
Coarse salt and freshly ground pepper
Freshly grated nutmeg
½ teaspoon baking powder
½ teaspoon cuminseed
½ teaspoon ground mustard seed
2 tablespoons ghee, page 45, or peanut oil

Leftover potatoes can be used. These go with most chicken and meat dishes, stews, roasts, or grilled meat.

• Mix the mashed potatoes with the remaining ingredients except the ghee. Shape the mixture into patties about 2½ inches in diameter. Fry in hot ghee and drain on paper towels. Use more ghee if necessary. Serves 4.

RICE

It is important not to overcook rice. It should be tested after 12 minutes of cooking. The grains should be soft without being either mushy or hard in the center.

The popular brands of rice available in supermarkets are not as good as Indian Patna rice or Italian rice. Instant rice is worthless. Use Patna for boiled rice dishes. The grain is thinner and absorbs less water. Italian rice is good for risotto because it absorbs more liquid.

Method 1

• Allow ⅓–½ cup of rice per person. Half fill a large pot with water, salt it, and bring to a boil. Add the rice gradually so that the water does not stop boiling. Stir with a fork and boil the rice rapidly, uncovered. Test after 12 minutes. It usually takes 15–20 minutes. When done, empty the rice into a colander and run under cold water. Melt some butter in a separate saucepan, add the rice, cover with a cloth, and leave for a few minutes (or up to half an hour). Alternatively you can melt some butter in a baking dish and put the rice into a slow oven until needed.

Half a lemon added to the boiling water keeps the rice white. Oil added prevents it from boiling over.

Method 2

• Allow 2½ cups liquid and 1 teaspoon salt for each cup of raw rice. Add 1 tablespoon butter to water and bring to a boil. Add rice gradually, cover, and reduce flame to low. Simmer for about 20 minutes, or until done. Use a tight-fitting cover.

PLAIN BOILED RICE, CHINESE-STYLE

1 *cup long-grained rice*
1¾ *cups cold water*

• Rinse rice under cold water. Put into a 2-quart saucepan and add the cold water. Bring to a boil. Stir, and when it reaches a rolling boil, cover tightly, reduce heat to low, and cook for 20 minutes. Turn off heat and let rice stand for 10 minutes. Serve hot. Serves 2.

SAFFRON RICE, CARIBBEAN-STYLE

1½ *cups rice*
1 *medium onion, chopped*
3 *tablespoons olive oil*
Pinch saffron
Coarse salt
2½ *cups chicken stock*

• Fry the onion in the oil until golden. Add the rice and saffron and fry for 5 minutes. Boil the stock, add it, and season with salt. Stir and cook over low heat for 15–20 minutes, covered. Stir occasionally. Serves 4.

ARROZ À LA MEXICANA (MEXICAN RICE)

- 1 *medium onion, coarsely chopped*
- 2 *cloves garlic, peeled*
- 4 *cups chicken stock*
- 4 *ripe tomatoes, peeled and chopped, page 34*
- ¼ *cup olive oil*
- 2 *cups white rice*
- *Coarse salt and freshly ground pepper*
- 1 *cup peas (if frozen peas are used, they should first be thawed)*
- *Red and green fresh chili peppers, pages 27–29*
- *Fresh coriander*
- 1 *avocado*
- *Fresh lemon or lime juice*

This is good with Mexican dishes or grilled fish, meat, or chicken.

• Put the onion and the garlic in a blender with ½ cup chicken stock and the tomatoes. Blend until smooth.

Heat the oil in a large saucepan. Fry the rice until opaque. Add the tomato mixture, peas, and the remaining stock. Season with salt and pepper. Simmer, covered, until nearly all the liquid is absorbed.

Cut the chilies from tip down to stem in strips so that they form flowers. Garnish the rice with the chilies, coriander sprigs, and peeled and sliced avocado on which you have squeezed lemon or lime juice to prevent it from turning brown. Serves 6.

ARROZ VERDE (MEXICAN GREEN RICE)

- 4 *poblano chilies, peeled and coarsely chopped, pages 27–29*
- 4 *cups chicken stock*
- 1 *cup chopped fresh parsley or coriander*
- 1 *medium onion, coarsely chopped*
- 1 *clove garlic, peeled*
- *Coarse salt and freshly ground pepper*
- ¼ *cup olive oil*
- 2 *cups long-grain rice*

Serve with Mexican food, chicken, fish, and grilled meats. Bell peppers plus a teaspoon of ground dried chilies may be substituted for poblano chilies.

• Combine ½ cup stock and remaining ingredients except oil and rice in a blender. Reduce to smooth purée. Set aside.

Pour oil in heavy casserole and when hot add the rice. Stir until the grains become opaque. Add the chili mixture and the remaining stock which you have brought to a boil in a separate pan. Simmer for about 20 minutes, or until rice has absorbed all the liquid. Serves 4–6.

MOORS AND CHRISTIANS (CARIBBEAN BEANS AND RICE)

- *2 tablespoons olive oil*
- *1 clove garlic, chopped*
- *1 medium onion, chopped*
- *1 green bell pepper, chopped*
- *1½ cups long-grain white rice*
- *Coarse salt and freshly ground pepper*
- *2 cups water*
- *2 cups cooked black beans*

Leftover black beans can be used for this recipe (see page 151 for Mexican Beans).

• Heat the oil in a heavy saucepan and fry the garlic, onion, and pepper until soft but not browned. Add the rice, fry for a couple of minutes until opaque, add the water, beans, and seasonings. Cover and simmer over low heat until all the water has been absorbed (about 20 minutes). Serves 4.

PEAS AND RICE

- *2 medium onions, chopped*
- *2 tablespoons ghee, page 45, or butter*
- *1 tablespoon cardamom seeds*
- *2-inch cinnamon stick*
- *1½ cups rice*
- *1 pound peas (podded fresh or frozen)*
- *4 cups boiling water*

This always looks attractive and can be served with any curry or main dish.

• Fry the onions in the ghee without browning. Add the cardomom seeds, cinnamon, and rice. Fry for 7 minutes. Add the peas and cook for 3 minutes, stirring constantly to prevent burning. Add the water and cook, covered, for about 30 minutes, or until rice is done. Serves 4–6.

KITCHIRI (RICE AND LENTILS)

- 3 *cups rice*
- ½ *pound lentils*
- *Coarse salt*
- 6 *cups water*
- 4 *tablespoons ghee, page* 45, *or butter*
- ½ *tablespoon cuminseed*

This is a traditional accompaniment for curries. A bowl of yoghurt and a bowl of lemon or mango pickles go well with it.

• Rinse the rice and the lentils and cook in boiling salted water until soft. Drain thoroughly. Melt the ghee, stir in the cuminseed, and pour the mixture over the rice and lentils. Serves 6.

BHUGIA

- 1 *cup plain white flour*
- 1 *teaspoon turmeric*
- ¼ *teaspoon ground chili*
- 2 *scallions, minced*
- 2 *chilies, minced*
- 2 *eggs*
- *Coarse salt*
- *Freshly ground pepper*
- ¼ *cup chopped cooked vegetables (peas, carrot, cauliflower, etc.)*
- *Oil for deep-frying*

Served with Indian meals, these are golden puffs, rather like doughnuts in appearance but without the hole in the middle. Make the batter in advance and cook them at the last minute so that they are hot when served.

• Mix the flour with the turmeric, ground chili, scallions, chilies, and add the eggs. Mix well, season with salt and pepper, and if too dry moisten with a little milk. Stir in the vegetables.

Heat oil in a deep-fryer and when hot drop the batter in by tablespoons. Drain on paper and keep hot. Serves 4–6.

CHAPATTIS

- 1 *pound whole-wheat flour (do not use white)*
- *Pinch salt*
- 1 *cup water (approximately)*

These Indian breads are easy to make and go well with curry. Leave the dough for half an hour in a warm place before you roll it out.

• Mix the flour and the salt. Put the mixture on a pastry board and make a well in the middle. Add the water, a little at a time, until dough becomes elastic, and knead until smooth (5 to 10 minutes). Cover with a damp cloth and allow dough to rest for half an hour.

Knead the dough lightly, mold it into small balls (about 1½ inches in diameter), and roll out as thin as possible. Dust with flour. Heat a heavy-bottomed skillet or griddle (with no fat in it) and fry the chapattis for two minutes on each side. When the bread puffs up it is ready. Serve with butter.

SAMOSA (INDIAN PASTRY TURNOVER)

- *4 cups plain white flour*
- *4 tablespoons ghee, page 45, or butter*
- *¾ tablespoons salt*
- *Yoghurt or sour milk as needed to make a dough*
- *Stuffing (see paragraph at right)*
- *Oil for deep-frying*

These turnovers are delicious hot or cold (better hot) and can be served as an appetizer or with a main course. You can vary the stuffing. Most common is a mixture of mashed potatoes, chopped green peas, chopped chives, parsley, and mint, paprika, and salt moistened with lime juice. Ground beef or lamb which has been cooked with garlic and onions and flavored with chopped parsley, mint, and chives is also popular.

• Sift the flour and work in the melted ghee. Season with salt, knead in the yoghurt, beginning with about ½ cup, until you have a stiff but pliable dough. Shape into small balls and roll out into circles about 2 inches in diameter. Place a spoonful of stuffing in each circle, wet the edges and roll over the other half, press down, and deep-fry in oil until golden. Drain on paper towels. Serves 6–8.

HUNGARIAN DUMPLINGS

- *1½ cups all-purpose flour*
- *3 tablespoons coarse salt*
- *2 eggs*
- *½ cup milk*
- *1 stick butter, melted*
- *About 2 quarts boiling water*

Serve these with Roast Chicken with Paprika, page 98, Székely Gulyás, page 115, Hungarian Pork Chops, page 119, or Hungarian Veal Goulash, page 122.

• Sift the flour into a bowl with the salt. Beat the eggs and add with the milk and 1 tablespoon of the melted butter. Mix thoroughly so that there are no lumps. Drop a spoonful at a time into the boiling water and cook until the dumplings rise to the surface (about 8–10 minutes). Drain thoroughly, put in a warm bowl, and pour remaining melted butter over them. Keep warm until ready to serve. Serves 4.

DHAL

1 *pound lentils*
½ *teaspoon turmeric*
½ *teaspoon chili powder*
2 *medium onions, chopped*
1 *tablespoon ghee, page* 45, *or butter*
4 *tomatoes, peeled and chopped, page* 34
Coarse salt and freshly ground pepper

This Indian lentil dish should have the consistency of a thick sauce.

• Simmer the lentils in water to cover with the turmeric and chili powder. Meanwhile, cook the onion in the butter and add the tomatoes. Simmer gently for about 10 minutes.

Add the tomato-onion mixture to the cooked lentils, season with salt and pepper, and serve. Serves 4.

JALAPEÑO CORN BREAD

very good

2½ *cups yellow cornmeal*
1 *cup white flour*
2 *tablespoons sugar*
1 *tablespoon coarse salt*
4 *tablespoons baking powder*
3 *eggs*
1½ *cups milk*
½ *cup peanut oil*
2 *cups canned creamed corn*
8 *jalapeño chilies, chopped, pages* 27–29
2 *cups grated sharp Cheddar cheese*
1 *medium onion, grated*

Serve with Mexican food or with grilled meat or fish.

• Combine the cornmeal, flour, sugar, salt, and baking powder in a mixing bowl. Beat the eggs, add the milk, peanut oil, and stir in the creamed corn. Add the chilies, cheese, and onion. Stir into the flour mixture and pour into 2 oiled 9 × 11-inch pans. Bake in a preheated 425-degree oven until done (about 25 minutes). Makes 2.

SALADS

It seems to have become an American tradition to start a meal with a lump of iceberg lettuce accompanied by a pale pink, floury slice of tomato, the whole thing smeared with a concoction that goes under the heading of Roquefort dressing but looks like library paste. This cloying dish is supposed to stimulate the appetite for the entrée.

Salad is best served after, not before, the main course. There are, however, certain mixed salads which are good as hors d'oeuvres. This chapter contains several such salads, raw or cooked, all of them spicy, that are also excellent lunch dishes. They are interesting in buffet spreads too.

Plain green salads and light salads to be served after spicy foods are also included here. The freshest, ripest ingredients should be used. Vegetables should be washed and dried with dish cloths unless they are organically grown and clean. Lettuce should be torn into strips, other vegetables chopped the same size. Bottled dressings are an anathema.

GREEN SALAD

• Fresh green leafy vegetables only should be used in this salad. These may include lettuce, spinach leaves, endive, watercress, dandelion leaves, arugola, young escarole, diced fennel, green bell peppers, thinly sliced cucumbers, or broccoli divided into small flowerets. Fresh green herbs such as basil, mint, tarragon, chives, parsley, or coriander are excellent—but dried herbs won't do.

A basic dressing is the vinaigrette, that should be poured over the salad shortly before serving. Combine 2 tablespoons tarragon or red wine vinegar with 6 tablespoons olive oil, ¼ teaspoon prepared Dijon-type mustard, a crushed garlic clove (if you like), coarse salt, and freshly ground black pepper. Toss the salad thoroughly, correct seasoning, let stand for a minute or two, and then serve.

RICE SALAD

3 cups hot cooked rice
4 tomatoes, peeled and chopped, page 34
2 green bell peppers, chopped
1 diced chili, chopped
1 tablespoon chopped fresh parsley, chives, or coriander.
Other ingredients according to taste:
chopped bottled pimientos
diced raw mushrooms
cooked green peas
chopped olives
chopped cucumber
chopped hardboiled egg
paprika

This salad is good with spicy grilled meat or fish.

• Combine the rice with a vinaigrette sauce (see under Green Salad, page 163) and add the remaining ingredients. Toss, cool, and serve at room temperature. Serves 4.

MOROCCAN FENNEL SALAD

1 pound fennel hearts
¼ teaspoon ground cumin
½ teaspoon paprika
¼ cup olive oil
Juice of ½ lemon
1 teaspoon mustard
Coarse salt and freshly ground pepper

• Slice the fennel into very thin rounds. Combine the remaining ingredients, correct seasoning, and pour onto the fennel. Toss and serve. Serves 4.

Note: Moroccan salads are generally served at the beginning of a meal.

KIM CHEE (KOREAN PICKLED CABBAGE)

1 head Chinese cabbage
2 tablespoons coarse salt
4 scallions
1 clove garlic
2 hot chilies, finely chopped
Dash Tabasco
½-inch piece ginger, grated

This is Korea's national dish. It is very good with broiled or stir-fried meats and chicken. Rice is the other side dish to serve along with this pickled cabbage.

Chinese cabbage is available in many supermarkets nowadays, besides Chinese and specialty stores. Kim chee can also be bought canned.

• Chop the cabbage coarsely and salt it. Let stand for an hour, then rinse it under cold water to remove the salt.

Shred the scallions, mince the garlic, and add to the cabbage with the chilies, Tabasco, and ginger. Place the mixture in a glass or earthenware jar and add water to cover. Leave for 1 to 5 days in the lower part of the refrigerator. Serve at room temperature. This pickled cabbage can be stored in a sealed jar in the refrigerator. Serves 8.

BEAN SPROUT SALAD WITH MUSTARD DRESSING

1 *pound fresh bean sprouts*
1 *tablespoon powdered mustard*
2 *tablespoons soy sauce*
1 *teaspoon sugar*
2 *tablespoons white wine vinegar or cider vinegar*
½ *cup sesame or mustard oil*

Serve this salad with Chinese meals or with broiled chicken, fish, or meat.

• Wash the bean sprouts and pour boiling water over them. Drain. Set aside.

Combine the remaining ingredients and pour the mixture on the bean sprouts. Toss well and let stand for an hour before serving. Serves 4.

Note: This mustard dressing is very good with cold chicken. Use half the amount of oil.

ASINAN (INDONESIAN VEGETABLE SALAD)

Vegetables
½ *pound fresh bean sprouts, steamed for 1 minute*
½ *pound shredded green cabbage*
1 *cucumber, thinly sliced*
1 *bunch radishes, thinly sliced*
3 *cakes bean curd, cubed*
1 *cup chopped roasted unsalted peanuts*

Dressing
3 *hot fresh chilies, minced, pages 27–29*
½ *teaspoon minced fresh ginger*
1 *clove garlic, finely chopped*
2 *tablespoons sugar*
¼ *cup vinegar*
2 *cups water*
½ *teaspoon trassi, page 24*
Coarse salt and freshly ground pepper

• Arrange vegetables in a mound on a large plate. Mix the chilies, ginger, garlic, sugar, and vinegar in an electric blender until a smooth purée. Add the water and the trassi and blend for a few seconds more. Season with salt and pepper. Pour over the salad and serve. Serves 4.

GADO GADO
(COOKED INDONESIAN VEGETABLE SALAD)

Vegetables

2 *bean curd cakes, cubed and deep-fried in peanut oil until crisp*
6 *small new potatoes, cooked*
1 *pound string beans, steamed*
1 *pound spinach, steamed*
1 *pound bean sprouts, blanched*
2 *cucumbers, thinly sliced, with skins (unless the skins have been paraffin-waxed)*
2 *hardboiled eggs*

Sauce

3 *tablespoons peanut oil*
1 *medium onion, chopped*
3 *cloves garlic, chopped*
1 *teaspoon trassi paste, page* 24
2 *fresh chilies, coarsely chopped, pages* 27–29
4 *cups roasted unsalted peanuts*
½ *teaspoon laos powder, page* 24
1 *teaspoon minced fresh ginger*
4 *cups Coconut Milk, page* 44
3 *tablespoons brown sugar*
¼ *cup Tamarind Water, page* 45
Coarse salt to taste
Lemon juice to taste

The vegetables should be slightly crisp after steaming. Do not overcook them.

• Heat the oil in a deep, heavy-bottomed frying pan. Cook the onions and garlic for 5 minutes without burning. Add the trassi, blend, and put the mixture in a blender with the chilies and peanuts. Blend at high speed, using a little coconut milk to moisten if necessary. Add the laos powder, ginger, coconut milk, sugar, and tamarind water. Blend until smooth. Return to skillet. Bring to a boil and simmer for about 15 minutes, or until sauce is consistency of heavy cream. Add salt, lemon juice, correct seasoning, and pour over the vegetables. Garnish with chopped scallions if you like. The sauce may also be served separately in a sauceboat. Serves 6–8.

MOROCCAN GREEN PEPPER AND TOMATO SALAD

4 tomatoes, prepared according to page 34
3 green bell peppers, prepared according to page 34
1 tablespoon chopped fresh green chilies, pages 27–29
3 tablespoons olive oil
½ teaspoon cumin
Coarse salt and freshly ground pepper
Juice of 1 lemon
½ Moroccan Preserved Lemon, page 187
2 tablespoons chopped parsley

Don't bother to make this if you can't get ripe, juicy tomatoes.

• Arrange the vegetables and chopped chilies in a dish. Combine the oil, cumin, salt, pepper, lemon juice, and pour over. Chop the skin of the preserved lemon, sprinkle on with the parsley. Serve at room temperature. Serves 4.

SAALOUK (MOROCCAN EGGPLANT SALAD)

2 pounds eggplant
3 zucchini
Olive oil for frying
2 green bell peppers, prepared according to page 34
2 small fresh green chilies, prepared according to page 29
3 tomatoes, peeled, seeded, and diced
3 cloves garlic
2 teaspoons cumin
1 teaspoon paprika
2 tablespoons fresh chopped coriander
Juice of 1 lime or lemon

This salad is like a spicy ratatouille and should be served as an appetizer.

• Cut the eggplant into slices ½-inch thick, salt, and let drain in a colander for 30 minutes. Slice the zucchini. Heat the oil in a heavy frying pan and fry the eggplant and zucchini until lightly browned. Remove with a slotted spoon and reserve the oil.

Mash the eggplant and zucchini with the bell peppers, chilies, tomatoes, garlic, cumin, paprika, coriander, salt, pepper, and lemon juice. Add the oil. Correct seasoning. Serve at room temperature. Serves 4.

TURKISH CUCUMBERS IN YOGHURT

- 2 *cucumbers*
- *Coarse salt*
- 1 *cup plain yoghurt*
- 2 *cloves garlic, minced*
- *Freshly ground black pepper*
- 1 *tablespoon fresh chopped dill or mint (optional)*

This salad is an antidote to hot, spicy dishes.

• Peel the cucumbers and slice thinly. Salt them and let them stand for half an hour. Pat them dry with paper towels. Mix the yoghurt with garlic, pepper, and dill. Correct seasoning and pour over the cucumbers. Toss well and serve chilled. Serves 4.

YOGHURT CUCUMBER SALAD

- 2 *cucumbers*
- *Coarse salt*
- ½ *cup yoghurt*
- 1 *tablespoon vinegar or lemon juice*
- 1 *clove garlic, chopped*
- *Freshly ground pepper*
- *Fresh chopped mint or basil*

A very cooling salad to serve with hot curries. It can be eaten separately or together with a curry.

• Peel the cucumbers and slice thinly. Salt them and let stand for about half an hour. Squeeze out the excess moisture with paper towels. Combine the yoghurt, vinegar, garlic, and pepper and toss the cucumber in this mixture. Correct seasoning, sprinkle with herbs, and chill until ready to eat. Serves 4.

MIDDLE EASTERN CHICK PEA SALAD

- 3 *cups chick peas (or 2 10-ounce cans)*
- ½ *cup olive oil*
- 3 *tablespoons vinegar*
- *Lemon juice to taste*
- *Coarse salt and freshly ground pepper*
- 1 *clove garlic, finely chopped (optional)*
- 1 *medium onion, chopped*
- 1 *cup chopped vegetables (celery, tomatoes, peppers, or all three)*
- 2 *tablespoons diced pimientos*
- *Fresh chopped parsley to garnish*

Although I normally disdain canned foods, the effort and time required to cook dried chick peas is hardly worth it. The canned ones are very good but they should be rinsed thoroughly and heated to absorb the dressing.

This is a good salad to serve with lamb, curries, and Indian meals. It can also be served on lettuce leaves with tomatoes, peppers, pimientos, and celery.

• Heat the chick peas and drain them. Mix the oil with the vinegar, lemon juice, salt, and pepper. Add the garlic and the onions and toss the warm chick peas thoroughly with the mixture. Add the vegetables, mix in, and arrange the pimientos on top of the salad. Sprinkle with parsley. Serves 4.

MUSTARD SPINACH SALAD

- 1 *pound young spinach*
- ½ *cup olive oil*
- 2 *tablespoons Dijon-type mustard*
- 3 *tablespoons red wine vinegar*
- ½ *Spanish onion, finely chopped*
- *Squeeze of lemon juice to taste*
- *Coarse salt*
- *Freshly ground pepper*

This is a good salad to serve after lamb or chicken dishes.

• Wash the spinach thoroughly in several changes of water. Remove tough stems, dry the leaves well, and refrigerate until ready to use.

Combine the oil with the remaining ingredients and mix well. Pour the dressing over the spinach, toss, and serve. Serves 4.

PAPRIKA SALAD WITH LEMON DRESSING

Salad

- 2 *tart apples*
- 2 *stalks celery*
- 1 *orange*
- 1 *cup halved, shelled walnuts*
- 1 *head Boston lettuce*

Dressing

- *Juice of half a lemon*
- ¼ *teaspoon grated lemon peel*
- ½ *teaspoon dry mustard*
- 1 *tablespoon dark prepared mustard*
- 1 *tablespoon Hungarian paprika*
- ¼ *cup walnut oil*
- *Coarse salt*
- ½ *cup heavy cream*

• Peel and chop the apples. Chop the celery, peel and chop the orange, and combine in a salad bowl with the walnuts. Wash and dry the lettuce, tear into strips, and add. In another bowl combine all the dressing ingredients except the cream. Little by little, beat the cream into the dressing. Season with salt and pour over the salad. Toss and serve. Serves 4.

SAUCES & MARINADES

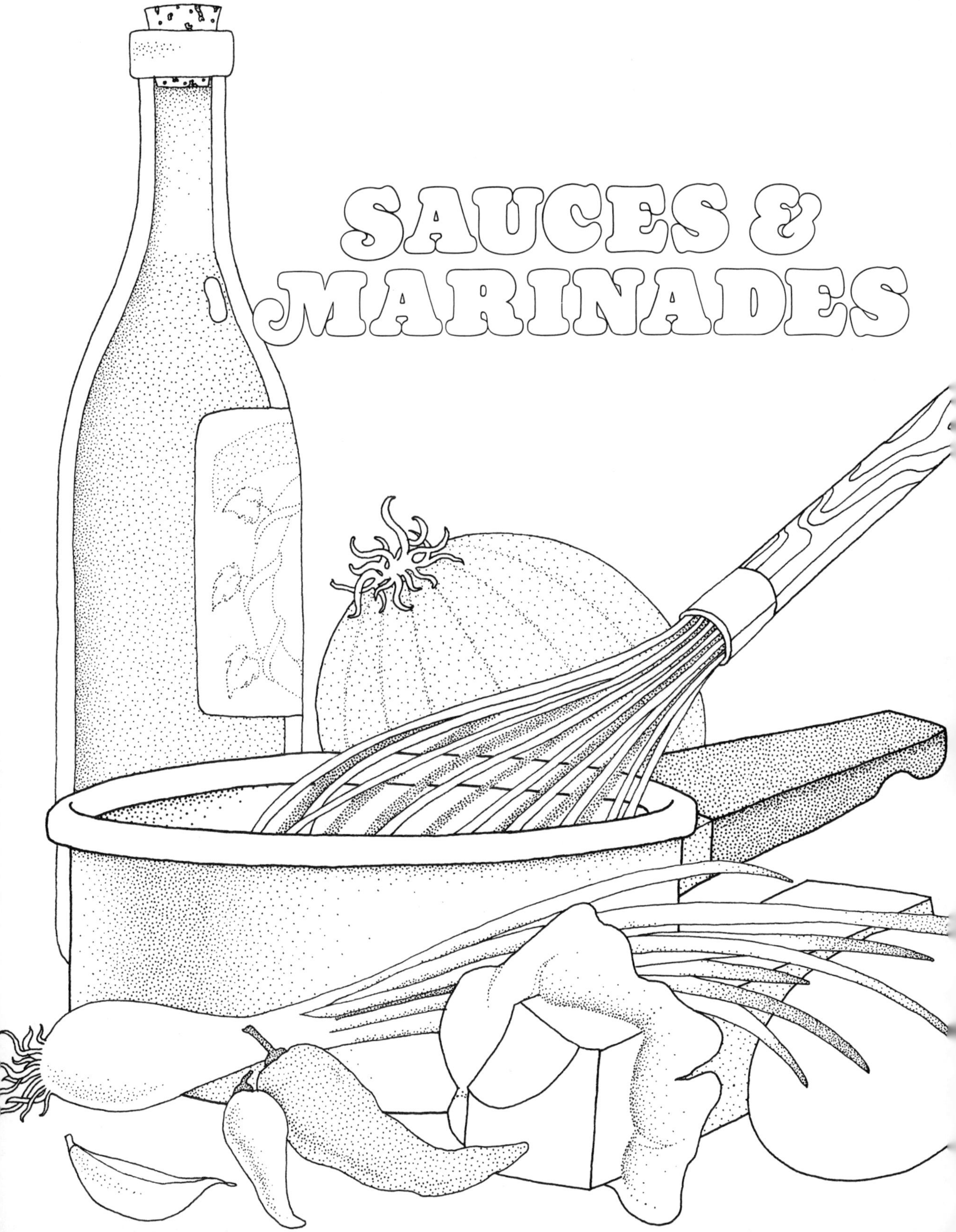

Epicurean cooks sharpen with cloyless sauce
his appetite.

—*Anthony and Cleopatra*

An ordinary piece of meat or fish can be transformed by its sauce. Sauces are extremely important in hot, spicy cuisines. Some may be "on the table" sauces which can be made and kept in a sealed jar under refrigeration for about a week, sometimes longer. Others are freshly made. See the chapter on relishes for Indonesian sambals, which are a distant relative of Mexican table sauces.

Cold sauces can be set out in small bowls or used as dips. They are delicious with cold meat.

This chapter also has a section on marinades that will make meat more tender and improve its taste. Meat can be kept for up to a week in a marinade (Indians say meat marinated in mustard oil will keep for months but I haven't tried it). Even fish can be kept for a couple of days in a marinade, at room temperature in cool weather. By using a marinade you can avoid freezing meat or fish, and enhance their flavor.

SAUCES

DEVIL SAUCE

4 *tablespoons butter*
2 *shallots, chopped*
2 *green chilies, chopped*
2 *slices fresh ginger, chopped*
2 *cups homemade stock (beef or chicken)*
1 *cup red wine*
1 *tablespoon red wine vinegar*
2 *tablespoons chutney*
1 *tablespoon red currant jelly*

• Melt the butter in a saucepan and cook the shallots, chilies, and ginger until the shallots are soft. Add the stock and wine and bring to a boil. Season with remaining ingredients and serve with tongue or ham. Makes about 2½ cups.

ROUILLE

4 dried hot peppers
Hot water to cover
5 cloves garlic, peeled
Coarse salt
Olive oil

This is served as an accompaniment to bouillabaisse or jellied bouillabaisse.

• Soak the peppers in the hot water for at least 2 hours. Drain and mash in a mortar and pestle with the garlic and salt. Work the oil in slowly until the sauce is the consistency of mustard. If you like, the rouille may be thinned with bouillabaisse broth. Makes about 1–1½ cups.

NEWBURG SAUCE

3 tablespoons butter
3 tablespoons white flour
1 teaspoon Hungarian paprika
2 cups light cream
3 egg yolks, beaten
1 tablespoon dry sherry
Coarse salt and freshly ground white pepper

Serve this with cooked lobster, crab, prawns, or scallops.

• Melt the butter in a saucepan. Add the flour and cook for a couple of minutes taking care to prevent burning. Add the paprika, cook for a minute, then add the cream. Bring to a boil, stirring, and turn down heat. Beat in the egg yolks, taking great care not to maintain too high a heat or they will curdle. Add the sherry, season with salt and pepper, and use either as a separate sauce or add the shellfish to the sauce and heat through. Makes about 1½ cups.

HORSERADISH SAUCE

4 tablespoons butter
1 medium onion, finely chopped
4 tablespoons flour
½ cup grated horseradish
2 cups beef or chicken stock
Coarse salt
Freshly ground white pepper
1 teaspoon sugar
½ cup sour cream or heavy cream

Serve this sauce with boiled or corned beef. It is a popular sauce in Russian and Viennese cooking.

• Melt the butter in a heavy-bottomed saucepan. Fry the onion gently without browning it. Stir in the flour and cook for a few minutes without browning. Add the horseradish, stir in, then add the stock, salt, pepper, and sugar. Beat with a wire whisk until the sauce becomes thick and smooth. Stir in the cream, heat through (without boiling), correct seasoning, and serve. Makes about 2 cups.

MUSTARD SAUCE

- 1 *tablespoon butter*
- 1 *tablespoon olive oil*
- 1 *medium onion, finely chopped*
- *Parsley sprigs*
- 1 *tablespoon flour*
- 1 *cup fish, chicken, or meat stock*
- 1 *cup dry white wine*
- 3 *tablespoons Dijon-type mustard*
- *Coarse salt and freshly ground pepper*

Good with fish, ham, and pork.

• Heat butter and oil in a saucepan. Add onion and parsley and fry until onion is soft, without browning. Sprinkle with flour, cook, stirring, for 2 minutes. Add stock and wine and bring to a boil. Simmer for 20 minutes.

Strain the sauce into the top of a double boiler. Add the mustard, stir well, and cook until thick and smooth. Season with salt and pepper. Makes approximately 2 cups.

EGG AND MUSTARD SAUCE FOR HAM

- 3 *eggs*
- 2 *tablespoons white wine*
- ½ *cup sour cream*
- 2 *teaspoons Dijon-type mustard*
- *Coarse salt*
- *Freshly ground white pepper*

The trick to making this French sauce is to use a double boiler or a trivet. If it gets too hot the eggs will curdle and your sauce will be ruined. Serve the sauce either separately with baked country ham or over ham slices.

• Beat the eggs until thick and whip with a wire whisk in a small saucepan (or top of double boiler). Beat in the wine. Over low heat, add the sour cream gradually, beating constantly, and the mustard. Season with salt and pepper, and when heated through and smooth remove from heat and serve immediately. Makes about 1 cup.

HUNGARIAN SAUCE

- 2 *tablespoons lard or bacon fat*
- 1 *medium onion, finely chopped*
- 1 *tablespoon flour*
- 1 *tablespoon Hungarian paprika*
- 1 *cup dry white or red wine*
- 1 *cup chicken or fish stock*
- *Herb bouquet (parsley, thyme, bay leaf, tied in cheesecloth)*
- 1 *cup sour cream*
- *Coarse salt*
- *Freshly ground pepper*

Use with fish, veal, or chicken.

• Heat the fat in a saucepan and fry the onion until golden. Stir in the flour and cook for 2–3 minutes. Add paprika, salt, and pepper. Add the wine, stock, and herb bouquet, and cook until thick. Add the sour cream, bring to a boil, and serve hot. Makes about 2½ cups.

SAUCE DIJONNAISE

4 hardboiled eggs
5 tablespoons Dijon-type mustard
Coarse salt
Freshly ground white pepper
1 cup olive oil
Juice of 1 lemon
1 tablespoon chopped capers
1 tablespoon chopped chives
1 tablespoon chopped fresh tarragon
Dash paprika

For cold fish, especially cold salmon.

• Sieve the egg yolks and set the whites aside. Combine the yolks with the mustard and season with salt and pepper. Beat together and then add the oil, drop by drop, beating it in as for a mayonnaise. Beat in the lemon juice, then add the remaining ingredients. To serve, spread over the fish and decorate with chopped whites and paprika. Makes about 1½ cups.

SOFRITO (PUERTO RICO)

½ pound salt pork, finely diced
2 tablespoons Achiote Oil, page 43, or 1 tablespoon annatto seeds
4 medium onions, finely chopped
4 cloves garlic, finely chopped
2 green bell peppers, finely chopped
½ pound lean boneless ham, diced
4 tomatoes, coarsely chopped
1 tablespoon fresh coriander, chopped
1 teaspoon oregano
Coarse salt and freshly ground black pepper

The Spaniards brought this to the Caribbean, where it is now used as a basic cooking sauce. It can be made in large quantities and keeps for several weeks refrigerated, for several months frozen.

• Fry the salt pork in a heavy skillet. Remove with slotted spoon. Add the oil. If using seeds, fry them in the pork fat for 5 minutes, then remove. Add onions, garlic, and peppers and cook, stirring frequently, for 5 minutes. Add the ham, tomatoes, coriander, oregano, salt, and pepper. Stir and simmer, covered, for 20 minutes. Correct seasoning and store in tightly covered jars. Makes about 2 cups.

SAUCE CREOLE (MARTINIQUE)

1 *cup tomato purée*
Juice of 2 limes
1 *medium onion, finely chopped*
1 *tablespoon chopped celery*
1 *hot chili, chopped, pages 27–29*
4 *pimiento-stuffed olives, sliced*
Coarse salt and freshly ground pepper

This is delicious with broiled fish, crayfish, or lobster. It keeps for a week.

• Combine all ingredients in a bowl. Serve at once or cover tightly and store in refrigerator. Makes 1½ cups.

TOMATO SAUCE

2 *tablespoons butter*
2 *cloves garlic, finely chopped*
8 *large ripe tomatoes, peeled and chopped, page 34*
1 *teaspoon Worcestershire sauce*
1 *teaspoon Dijon-type mustard*
Dash Cayenne pepper
1 *teaspoon sugar*
Coarse salt and freshly ground pepper
Freshly grated nutmeg

• Melt the butter in a saucepan and fry the garlic for 2 minutes without burning. Add the remaining ingredients and simmer until you have a thick purée, stirring frequently.

SALSA DE CHILE ROJO (RED CHILI SAUCE)

- *5 ancho chilies, fresh, or dried soaked for 30 minutes in 1 cup boiling water, pages 27–29*
- *3 pequín chilies, crumbled,*
- *3 tomatoes, peeled and chopped, page 34*
- *1 medium onion, coarsely chopped*
- *1 clove garlic, peeled*
- *¼ cup olive or peanut oil*
- *Coarse salt and freshly ground pepper*
- *½ teaspoon sugar*
- *2 tablespoons chopped fresh coriander or parsley*
- *1 tablespoon red wine vinegar*

This is the classic Mexican sauce that is served on the side with most meals.

• Combine chilies, tomatoes, onion, and garlic in a blender and blend to purée. Heat oil in a skillet and pour in the sauce. Season with salt and pepper; add sugar and coriander. Cook for 5 minutes, stirring. Remove from heat, stir in vinegar, and cool.

Makes 2 cups. Will keep for 4–5 days in refrigerator.

SALSA DE JITOMATE (MEXICAN TOMATO SAUCE)

- *2 tablespoons peanut or vegetable oil*
- *1 medium onion, finely chopped*
- *1 clove garlic, finely chopped*
- *4 large ripe tomatoes, peeled and chopped, page 34*
- *2 serrano chilies, chopped, pages 27–29*
- *Coarse salt and freshly ground pepper*
- *1 teaspoon sugar*
- *2 tablespoons chopped fresh coriander*

• Heat the oil and fry the onion and garlic without browning. Add the tomatoes, chilies, salt, pepper, and sugar, and simmer for about 15 minutes, or until you have a thick purée. Add the coriander, remove from heat, and serve hot or cold.

SALSA VERDE

- 1 *10-ounce can Mexican tomatoes*
- 2 *cloves garlic, peeled*
- 1 *onion, coarsely chopped*
- 2 *canned green chilies*
- ½ *cup coarsely chopped fresh coriander*
- *Coarse salt and freshly ground pepper*

Use as a dipping sauce for tortillas, to enliven soups, or with Tacos, page 63, Enchiladas, page 149, or Panuchos, page 64.

• Combine the tomatoes with their juice and remaining ingredients in a blender and purée. This sauce will keep for a week in a tightly covered jar. Makes 1½ cups.

SHORTCUT MOLE SAUCE

- 4 *tablespoons lard*
- 2 *medium onions, chopped*
- 6 *tomatoes, peeled and chopped, page 34*
- 2 *cloves garlic, chopped*
- 5–6 *teaspoons mole powder*
- *Coarse salt and freshly ground pepper*
- 2 *cups turkey or chicken stock*
- 2 *tablespoons sesame seeds*

Use with turkey, chicken, or pork. Mole powder is available in Mexican specialty stores. See Turkey Mole Poblano, page 105, for a regular mole poblano sauce.

• Heat the lard in a skillet and cook the onions until soft. Combine in an electric blender with the tomatoes and garlic. Add the mole powder, salt and pepper, and return to the skillet with the stock. Simmer for 45 minutes. Sprinkle with sesame seeds. Heat the meat through in the sauce before serving. Makes 2 cups.

YUCATÁN HOT PEPPER SAUCE

- 1 *medium onion, finely chopped*
- 1 *tomato, peeled, seeded, and chopped, page 34*
- 2 *canned serrano chilies, finely chopped, pages 27–29*
- ⅓ *cup orange juice*
- *Coarse salt*

This sauce appears on the table of every restaurant in Yucatán and is used with meals the way a North American might (unfortunately) use catchup. Use a little bit on the side of your plate (it is quite hot) to go with Mexican dishes, roast or grilled meat, chicken or fish. It is also very good with eggs.

• Combine all the ingredients in a small bowl. Makes 1 cup.

Note: The juice of Seville oranges is best here. If your orange juice is not tart enough, add a little lime or lemon juice.

PEBRE (CHILEAN HOT SAUCE)

1 tablespoon ground chili or Red Chili Paste, *page 42*
1 clove garlic, chopped
1 medium onion, chopped
1 bunch fresh coriander, chopped (parsley can be substituted)
1 tablespoon vinegar
2 tablespoons olive oil
½ cup water
Coarse salt to taste

Use this with meat and poultry. It is better than American bottled hot sauces, and is used by Chileans in much the same way. It will keep for 1 or 2 weeks in a sealed jar.

• Combine all the ingredients in a bowl, using the water to thin out the sauce. Leave for a couple of hours before using to develop the flavor. Makes about 1 cup.

MÔLHO DE PIMENTA E LIMÃO (BRAZILIAN PEPPER AND LEMON SAUCE)

4 bottled Tabasco peppers
1 medium onion, finely chopped
1 clove garlic, finely chopped
½ cup lemon juice
Coarse salt

Serve with feijoada completa or with pork sausages, corned beef, tongue, beef, or other cold meats.

• Combine all the ingredients and keep overnight or a few hours to marinate before serving.

CHINESE HOT CHILI DIP

2 cloves garlic, chopped
2 teaspoons Tabasco sauce
1 fresh or canned chili, chopped
½ cup soy sauce
1 teaspoon sugar

Use as a dipping sauce for fried shrimp, fish, lamb, beef, duck, or chicken. It is particularly good for deep-fried and barbecued food.

• Combine the ingredients and serve in a small shallow bowl. Makes about ¾ cup.

PEANUT SATÉ SAUCE

1 cup skinned roasted peanuts
2 tablespoons peanut oil
1 medium onion or 1/4 cup shallots, chopped
1 clove garlic, chopped
1 1/2–2 cups chicken stock
1 chili pepper, minced
1–1 1/2 tablespoons soy sauce (or ketjap manis, page 24)
1 tablespoon lime juice

This goes particularly well with Chicken Saté, page 104, for which it is the traditional accompaniment.

• Grind or blend the peanuts fine. Heat the oil in a skillet and fry the onion and the garlic without browning. Add the stock and bring to a boil. Add remaining ingredients and simmer for about 10 minutes. Thin out the sauce with more stock if necessary and serve hot. Makes 2 cups.

HOMEMADE MAYONNAISE

This is so superior to bought mayonnaise that it is well worth the effort of making at home. All you need is a little patience. You can make mayonnaise in the blender but I find my method works, it takes very little time, and you can do the beating while you are watching the evening news.

• I take an egg yolk and put it in a bowl with a little mustard. I beat it until it becomes thick and sticky. Then I tilt the bowl and add a very little olive oil. Keeping the bowl tilted so that the oil stays in one side of the bowl and isn't directly on the egg, I gradually beat it into the egg until it is completely absorbed. I continue adding oil this way, adding a little more as the egg begins to absorb it more easily. I then add lemon juice or vinegar and salt and more oil until I have the right consistency.

If it curdles I beat another egg yolk and add the curdled mixture to it bit by bit until it is smooth again. If your mixture curdles you have probably added too much oil too fast. Do not try to make mayonnaise on a very hot day.

Use about 4 yolks to a pint of oil. This will make about 2 cups. To lighten a mayonnaise add a little boiling water to it at the end.

PIQUANT MAYONNAISE

Mayonnaise, page 181 (about 1½ cups)
½ cup heavy cream
1 tablespoon prepared Dijon-type mustard
1 red bell pepper, diced
1 teaspoon Hungarian paprika
Coarse salt
Freshly ground white pepper

Use on hardboiled eggs, cold cooked vegetables, or with cold fish.

• Into the mayonnaise beat the cream, mustard, pepper, and paprika. Season with salt and pepper and put the mixture into a small bowl. Makes 2 cups.

MARINADES

ORANGE-CHILI MARINADE FOR PORK

• This is very good for chops and roasts. Combine 1 cup freshly squeezed orange juice, 2 tablespoons soy sauce, 1 tablespoon chili powder, ¼ cup olive oil, 1 teaspoon thyme, and freshly ground pepper. Pour onto the meat and marinate, turning occasionally. Pork can be kept for 5 days in this mixture.

YOGHURT-CURRY MARINADE FOR LAMB

• Lamb chops or leg of lamb become more tender and get a crispy skin after being marinated in this mixture. Combine 1 cup yoghurt with 1 tablespoon Mild Curry Powder, page 40, and 1 tablespoon coriander seed. Coat the meat and let stand for up to a week. The longer you leave it, the better the lamb will be.

YOGHURT-PAPRIKA MARINADE

• For lamb or veal, combine 1 cup yoghurt with 2 tablespoons Hungarian paprika. Lamb keeps for up to a week, veal for a couple of days.

MUSTARD-SEED–SOY-SAUCE MARINADE FOR LAMB

• This is great for leg of lamb. Combine 2 tablespoons Dijon-type mustard, 2 tablespoons mustard seed, ¼ cup soy sauce, ¼ cup olive oil. If you like, add ½ teaspoon rosemary. Coat the leg of lamb with this dressing and marinate for up to a week.

CHERMOULA (MOROCCAN MARINADE FOR FISH)

This marinade can be made hotter with extra crushed chili peppers or Cayenne pepper. Leave the fish to marinate for at least an hour so that the spices can penetrate it. The fish can then be baked in the oven or cooked on top of the stove.

For 4 pounds fish:

- *1 cup fresh coriander leaves*
- *4 cloves garlic, peeled*
- *2 tablespoons vinegar*
- *Juice of 1 lemon or lime*
- *1 tablespoon paprika*
- *1 tablespoon cumin*
- *½ teaspoon crushed chili*
- *Cayenne and coarse salt to taste*
- *2 tablespoons olive oil*

• Combine the ingredients in an electric blender and mix until smooth. For a better tasting marinade, work the coriander together with the garlic and vinegar with a mortar and pestle. Add the remaining ingredients and mix thoroughly.

PEPPER-WINE MARINADE FOR STEAK

This will make a tough steak tender. Cook the steak under low heat, first coating it with oil so that the juices will be sealed in. Slow cooking also helps to prevent toughening of meat—but this does not mean you need to overcook it.

For 2 medium-size steaks:

- *1 tablespoon fresh gingerroot, minced*
- *1 clove garlic, minced*
- *½ cup dry red wine*
- *1 tablespoon dark mustard*
- *1 tablespoon freshly ground black pepper*

• Combine all the ingredients and pour onto the steaks. Marinate overnight if possible, or at room temperature for a couple of hours. When ready to cook, remove the steaks from the marinade and dry them with paper towels. Coat them with oil and grill them. Meanwhile bring the marinade to a boil, and spoon resulting sauce over the steaks before serving.

YOGHURT–MUSTARD-SEED MARINADE FOR LAMB

- 1 *cup plain yoghurt*
- 1 *teaspoon crushed cardamom seed*
- ½ *teaspoon cumin*
- ½ *teaspoon ground allspice*
- 1 *tablespoon mustard seeds*
- ¼ *teaspoon mace*
- *Coarse salt and freshly ground pepper*

Lamb can be refrigerated in this mixture for up to a week. When roasted medium-rare it comes out remarkably tender.

For a 4–6 pound leg of lamb:

• Mix together all the ingredients and work into the lamb flesh. Turn the lamb occasionally in the mixture as it marinates. While it is roasting, pour a little oil onto the lamb.

CHINESE HOISIN-CHILI MARINADE FOR PORK

- 1 *tablespoon hoisin sauce*
- 1 *tablespoon chili sauce*
- 1 *inch fresh ginger, sliced*
- 2 *scallions, chopped*
- 2 *cloves garlic, chopped*
- ¼ *cup dry sherry*
- 2 *tablespoons soy sauce*
- 1 *tablespoon honey*
- *Coarse salt*
- *Freshly ground pepper*

This marinade is good for roasts and chops. Serve the cooked meat with rice or Chinese vegetables.

Hoisin sauce is available in Chinese specialty shops and some supermarkets.

• Combine all the ingredients and rub into the meat. Let stand overnight or for a couple of days. When cooking the meat, baste it with the marinade.

SENEGALESE MARINADE FOR MEAT, CHICKEN, OR FISH

- 4–5 *lemons*
- 1 *medium onion, minced*
- 2 *green chilies, minced, pages 27–29*
- *Coarse salt and freshly ground pepper*

This is excellent for grilled meat or fish. Leave the meat in the mixture for several hours. Grill over high heat, turning frequently, and serve with rice.

For 1½–2 pounds meat or fish:

• Combine ingredients, pour onto meat, and toss thoroughly. Let stand for a few hours at room temperature before cooking.

CHUTNEYS, PICKLES, RELISHES & CONDIMENTS

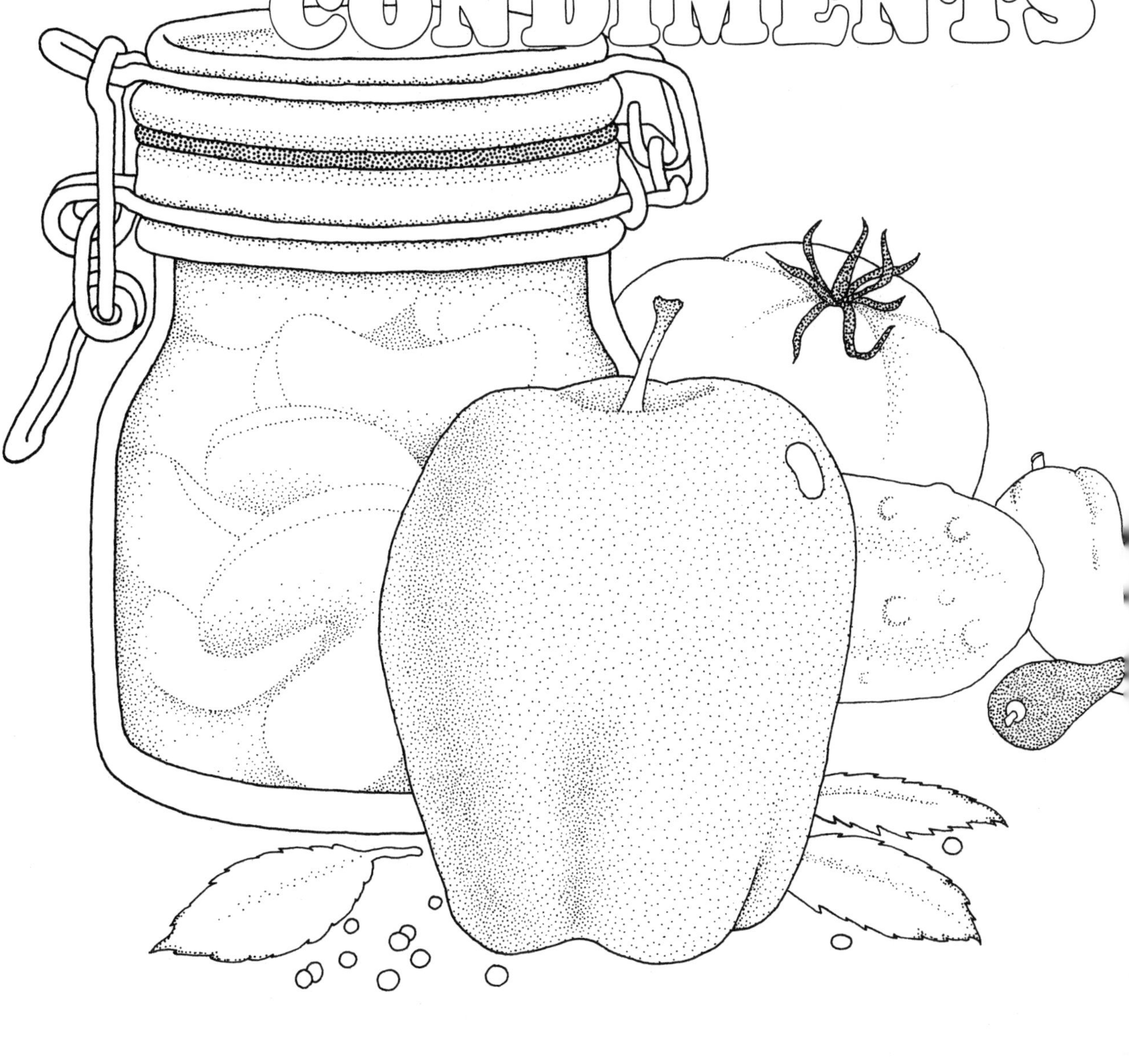

No Indian, Indonesian, or Mexican meal is complete without the traditional condiments. There is an astonishing diversity of chutneys and relishes in Indian and Pakistani cooking, ranging from mild and sweet to sharp and pungent in taste. Homemade chutneys are, of course, infinitely superior to bought ones and keep successfully in sealed jars away from the light. They improve over the months. I suggest that you make chutneys in fairly large quantities at a time since you may be surprised at how fast it goes.

Indonesian cooking, which is a mixture of sweet, sour, and hot flavors, is always accompanied by a fiery sambal. Remember that these dishes are supposed to be eaten with plenty of rice and in fairly small quantities. You may find that on their own they are far too hot.

Mustard is an important Western condiment and variations on that theme are extensive. Homemade mustard is delicious and keeps well.

Various spicy butters are included in this chapter. They can be used with meats and fish and also to spread on canapés for a different flavor.

MOROCCAN PRESERVED LEMONS

These lemons are used in Moroccan tajines (stews). They have no substitute.

6 *lemons*
Coarse salt
Cinnamon stick
5 *coriander seeds, whole*
5 *peppercorns, whole*
1 *bay leaf*
3 *cloves*
Lemon juice, as necessary

• Quarter the lemons, cutting down to within an inch of the bottom. Salt the pulp and reshape them. Put a layer of salt on the bottom of a glass pickling jar. Pack in the lemons, adding salt and remaining spices as you go. If the lemons are not covered by their own juice, squeeze some others and add the juice. Let stand for 30 days, tightly covered, and turn every day.

To use, remove as much as needed and rinse under cold running water. The lemons will keep for up to a year.

GREEN MANGO CHUTNEY

6 green mangoes
1 cup white wine vinegar
1 cup brown sugar
1 cup raisins
2-inch piece of fresh ginger
4 scallions

Green mangoes sometimes appear on the markets (they are always picked green for export) and they make an excellent chutney. This one is very easy to make and improves if it is left for several months before being used. It is a mild chutney and contains no chilies.

• With a sharp knife cut the skin and meat from the mango seeds (since the mangoes are unripe, the flesh does not peel away easily). Discard the seeds and chop the mangoes into small pieces. Combine the vinegar, sugar, and raisins in a saucepan and bring to a boil. Meanwhile, peel and slice the ginger into thin strips and chop the scallions. Add the mangoes, scallions, and ginger to the vinegar mixture and simmer, covered, for about half an hour, or until thick. Pour into a clean, warm, glass pickling jar and seal tightly. Makes 1 jar.

Note: I suggest you make four times the amount of this recipe at once. If you don't you may regret it later, not only because it is simpler to get the chutney making done all at one time, but green mangoes may not be for sale again for a while.

TOMATO CHUTNEY

2 pounds tomatoes, peeled and chopped, page 34
3 medium onions, chopped
1 cup vinegar
3 fresh red chilies, chopped, pages 27–29
3 cloves garlic, minced
½ teaspoon ground cumin
1 stick cinnamon
Juice of half a lemon
Coarse salt and freshly ground pepper
½ cup sugar

This chutney is excellent with cold ham.

• Put the tomatoes in a saucepan with the remaining ingredients except sugar. Bring to a boil and add the sugar. Simmer for 10–15 minutes, until chutney begins to thicken. Cool and store in sterile glass pickling jars.

CORIANDER AND COCONUT CHUTNEY

1 bunch coriander
2 medium onions, coarsely chopped
1-inch piece ginger, coarsely chopped
1 fresh chili
½ coconut, coarsely chopped
Juice of 1 lemon
¼ cup water
Coarse salt

Use fresh coriander only (available in Chinese, Latin American, and Indian grocers); do not substitute parsley. Once made, this will keep for a week.

• Trim the leaves from the coriander and put them in a blender with remaining ingredients. Blend and pour into a small bowl.

LEMON AND MUSTARD-SEED CHUTNEY

6 large lemons
4 medium onions
Coarse salt
2 cups white wine vinegar
4 tablespoons mustard seed
1 teaspoon ground allspice
1 pound light brown sugar
¼ pound raisins

This is a delicious chutney for fish or chicken. Limes may be used instead of the lemons.

• Slice the lemons (with peel) thinly, and peel and slice the onions. Place all on a large board or plate and sprinkle with salt. Let stand for a day.

Put the lemons and onions into a large heavy-bottomed saucepan with the remaining ingredients. Cover and simmer for about 45 minutes over low heat. Pour into warm, clean, glass pickling jars and seal.

INDIAN LIME PICKLE

12 limes
Juice of 3–4 limes
3 green chilies, prepared according to page 29
4 tablespoons green ginger, chopped
Coarse salt
Bay leaf

• Quarter the limes and remove the seeds. Salt the bottom of a glass pickling jar and arrange a layer of the limes, with any juices that may have run from them, adding a few chilies and pieces of ginger. Salt. Repeat until jar is full, then pour in lime juice and add bay leaf. Shake thoroughly. Let stand, tightly closed, for 30 days, turning once a day. This will keep for up to a year.

HARISSA (MOROCCAN HOT RELISH)

4 dried red chili peppers
2 cloves garlic, peeled
1 tablespoon caraway seeds
1 teaspoon ground cumin
1 teaspoon ground coriander seeds
Coarse salt
Olive oil

This relish is particularly good with black or green olives. Toss the olives in the mixture and serve as an hors d'oeuvre.

• Soak the peppers for an hour, drain them, and cut them small. In a mortar pound them with the garlic, caraway seeds, cumin, coriander, and salt. Put the mixture in a jar and cover with a layer of olive oil. It will keep for 2–3 months in a refrigerator.

SAMBAL KETJAP

• Use this Indonesian hot sauce with saté dishes, kebabs, and barbecued meats. If you cannot find ketjap in local specialty stores, use soy sauce instead.

Combine 1 cup ketjap with ⅓ cup fresh lime juice. Finely chop two fresh green chilies and mix in. Serve in a small bowl. Makes 1½ cups.

CHILI, ONION, AND TOMATO SAMBAL

1 tomato, diced
1 medium onion, diced
1 red chili, diced
1 green chili, diced
¼ cup fresh lime juice

The following sambals are traditional Indonesian condiments, all containing hot chilies. They are served in small bowls to accompany satés, and as relishes with Indonesian meals.

This chili, onion, and tomato sambal goes particularly well with beef, pork, or chicken satés, and with grilled or barbecued meats.

• Combine the ingredients in a small bowl and allow to marinate together for a couple of hours at room temperature before using. Makes about ¾ cup.

APPLE AND MINT SAMBAL

Finely chop two raw apples (with peel), a small bunch mint, 4 green chilies, and moisten with the juice of a lemon or lime.

Season with coarse salt. Will keep, refrigerated, for a couple of days.

Serve in a separate bowl with Indonesian dishes, curries, grilled or barbecued meat, fish, or poultry.

INDONESIAN HOT PEPPER RELISH

• In a blender combine 1 cup grated coconut, 2 red chili peppers, 1 medium onion (chopped), and the juice of a lime or lemon. A pestle and mortar may be used in place of a blender.

Use with Indonesian dishes, curries, barbecued lamb, or fish. Serve it in a small bowl.

INDONESIAN CUCUMBER RELISH

3 tablespoons sesame or peanut oil
1 medium onion, chopped
1 clove garlic, chopped
½ teaspoon crushed chili peppers
¼ teaspoon Cayenne pepper
½ teaspoon turmeric
½ teaspoon ground cuminseed
Coarse salt to taste
2 cucumbers, peeled and diced

This is good with oriental dishes, grilled meat, and satés. It will keep refrigerated for a couple of weeks.

• Heat the oil in a skillet and soften the onion with the garlic. Add remaining ingredients except cucumbers and cook for 10 minutes. Pour over the cucumbers and cool. Let stand overnight if possible before using.

HERB MUSTARD

You can buy this mustard ready-made but it is even better made at home. Use it with cold fish (especially salmon), chicken, beef, or ham. It has a lovely deep green color.

• In a blender combine 1 cup Dijon-type mustard with 2 tablespoons each chopped basil, parsley, tarragon, and chives. Blend until fine. Keep refrigerated in a tightly sealed jar.

PICKLED MUSTARD

Use with cold fish, chicken, stuffed eggs, beef, or sandwiches.

• Combine 1 cup Dijon-type mustard with 2 tablespoons each chopped capers, sweet pickles, and dill pickles. Moisten with 2 tablespoons dry white wine or beer. Keep in a tightly sealed jar in the refrigerator.

SPICED MUSTARD

2 large onions, chopped
2 cloves garlic, chopped
2 cups red wine vinegar
1 cup dry mustard
2 tablespoons coarsely ground mustard seed
½ teaspoon Cayenne
2 teaspoons coarse salt
Mustard oil

• Marinate the onions and garlic in the vinegar overnight. Strain the marinade and reserve. Combine the remaining ingredients except mustard oil in a bowl and mix with 1½ cups of the marinade. Pour the rest of the marinade into a saucepan. Bring to a boil and stir in the mustard paste. Simmer for 5 minutes. Cool. Stir in enough mustard oil to make a smooth paste. Pour into crocks or jars and cover tightly. Store in a cool place.

CHINESE MUSTARD

½ cup dry Chinese or English mustard
Boiling water

The Chinese make their mustard fresh before each meal because once made, if left for a long time, it loses flavor. Serve this in a small bowl with Chinese dishes. It is also good with beef.

Beer can be used instead of water (a good way to use up flat beer).

• Put the mustard in a small bowl and add the water until you have a smooth and rather runny paste. Leave for half an hour or so before using so that the mustard has time to develop its flavor.

DANISH MUSTARD

Use this on Danish open-face sandwiches, with herring, salmon, eggs, or beef. It is a hot mustard.

• Combine ½ cup dry mustard with 6 tablespoons light brown

sugar and add ¼ cup boiling water to make a paste. Beat in 3–4 tablespoons peanut or vegetable oil, 2 teaspoons Worcestershire sauce, and a teaspoon of white wine or cider vinegar. Set aside for an hour before using so that the flavor has time to develop.

DEVILLED BUTTER

1 stick softened butter
1 tablespoon Tabasco sauce
2 tablespoons Worcestershire sauce
1 teaspoon dry mustard
1 tablespoon minced onion or shallot
1 tablespoon chopped chives
1 tablespoon chopped parsley
Coarse salt and freshly ground pepper

• Mash the butter in a bowl and work in the remaining ingredients. Form into an oblong shape and refrigerate. Slice to serve.

BEURRE À L'INDIENNE

Use with chicken, lamb, or ham. It can also be used on grilled kidneys or as a spread for sandwiches or toast.

• Combine 1 stick softened butter with 1 teaspoon Mild Curry Powder, page 40, 1 teaspoon dry mustard, 1 tablespoon chopped mango chutney, dash Worcestershire sauce, dash Tabasco sauce, and lemon juice to taste. Season to taste with coarse salt and freshly ground pepper. Use at room temperature for spreading on bread. To serve with meat, shape into a cylinder or smooth out in a small bowl, and refrigerate for an hour or until ready to use.

MUSTARD BUTTER

Serve with ham, beef, or fish.

• Combine 1 stick softened butter with 2 tablespoons Dijon-type mustard. Add a little Cayenne and shape into a ball, or smooth out the mixture in a small bowl. Refrigerate for an hour before using.

PAPRIKA BUTTER

Use good Hungarian paprika or this will have no taste. It goes with grilled chicken, veal, or fish.

• Mince half an onion and sauté in a little butter. Add a tablespoon paprika and combine in a bowl with 1 stick softened butter. Sieve the mixture and refrigerate until ready to use.

INDEX

ABOUT THE AUTHOR

Ms. Hodgson, the daughter of a British Foreign Service officer, was educated in Lebanon, Sweden, Vietnam, and England. Presently, in addition to writing books and contributing articles to a wide variety of magazines (from *Hudson Review* to *Vogue*), she studies dance daily, and had a starring role in the soon-to-be-released short film called "A Parable for the Gods," based on a story by Jorge Borges.

She is a resident of New York City.